small spaces

Rebecca Tanqueray *photography by* Chris Everard

small spaces

MAKING THE MOST OF THE SPACE YOU HAVE

RYLAND
PETERS
& SMALL

LONDON NEW YORK

First published in 2003 by Ryland Peters & Small
20–21 Jockey's Fields, London WC1R 4BW
519 Broadway, 5th Floor, New York, NY 10012
www.rylandpeters.com
This compact edition published 2009

10 9 8 7 6 5 4 3 2 1

ISBN 978 1 84597 821 1

A CIP record for this book is available from the
British Library

The original US edition of this book was
catalogued as follows.

Library of Congress Cataloging-in-Publication Data
Tanqueray, Rebecca.
  Small spaces : making the most of the space you
have / Rebecca Tanqueray with photography by
Chris Everard.
    p. cm.
Includes index.
  ISBN 1-84172-414-9
  1. Small houses. 2. Interior decoration. I.
Everard, Chris. II.
Title.
  NA7115 .T26 2003
  747'.8837--dc21
                              2002014395

Printed and bound in China

designer Paul Tilby
senior editor Clare Double
location research Claire Hector
production Toby Marshall

production director Meryl Silbert
art director Leslie Harrington
publishing director Alison Starling

plans by Russell Bell

contents

introduction

Too many of us, these days, have too little space. With house prices everywhere escalating beyond our budgets, it's no surprise that we find ourselves squeezed into homes we've outgrown or forced to live somewhere smaller than we would like. Half the problem, of course, is that we have come to expect something more for our money. Bombarded by the media with images of loft apartments and giant open-plan living spaces, we are no longer content with our tiny homes, which – by comparison – seem cramped and claustrophobic.

Living in a small space, however, need not be a negative experience. Think of the Japanese, who have made an art out of it and who relish the positives of diminutive design. Approaching the space problem intelligently, they have come up with solutions which are compact and flexible, creating homes – or, at the extreme, capsule living spaces – that function brilliantly despite their size.

Here, too, we can do the same, and in this book I hope to encourage you to look again at your home – whether it is an urban flat or a country cottage – and to think of ways of overcoming its limitations. Of course, if you have the means, you may be able to change your space structurally by extending upwards or outwards or by knocking down walls to open up the interior. If this is not an option, however, there are many other methods of improving the feel of your home, by rearranging its layout, perhaps; investing in a few key pieces of furniture; or even just redecorating.

Browse through the case studies at the front of the book for inspiration. While at first sight some of these may seem far removed from your living quarters, all of them – from the dynamic mini skyscraper to the triangular Parisian apartment – illustrate countless innovative and accessible ways in which you can make the most of your space and offer ingenious ideas which have universal relevance. I've extrapolated the best of these in the second two sections – The Zones and Solutions – to show you just how easy it is to apply space-saving principles to every bit of your own home.

Who wants a loft when you can live somewhere compact, comfortable and cosy? Small spaces are the next big thing.

making the most of your space

Once an open space, the studio is now a multi-functional home. A mezzanine level was erected to serve as the bedroom and give access to a rooftop terrace. Exploiting vertical space like this is a good way of creating more room in any small home, as long as the ceilings are high enough.

LEFT The floor has been topped with resin and marble pebbles, giving the place the feel of an urban beach house. This adds textural interest to the otherwise neutral interior and is practical, providing a hard-wearing party-proof surface.

mezzanine magic

Most of us, when we buy a home, know just what we are getting: three bedrooms, one bathroom or whatever. Fashion photographer Guy Hills, however, had no such ready-made interior when he bought this old mews house in north London. A small two-storey building with unexpectedly high ceilings, it seemed perfect for a live-work space. The ground floor (undivided but for a couple of small rooms at the back) was just the place for Hills's photographic studio; upstairs – one large, undivided room with windows at front and back – could be his home.

Building an interior from scratch can be daunting, but it offers the opportunity to create somewhere tailor-made, somewhere that can accommodate just what you want, just where you want it. This is all very well and good in a large space but in a small one it can prove more of a challenge – particularly if, like Hills, you have big plans. Hills wanted his studio home to have all the usual living areas, but he wanted something more besides. 'I like a fairly minimal look,' he explains, 'so I needed acres of storage space. And I entertain a lot, so I needed room for lots of people.'

To help him turn his one room into a multi-functional living space he called in the experts, designer Maria Speake and

The living 'room' is defined only by its furniture: a curvy 1970s sofa, an armchair, a coffee table. Simple and masculine, this space is flexible enough to double as a meeting room when clients are visiting.

the space problem, not only because it took the 'bedroom' out of the main floor, freeing space for eating and entertaining, but also because it helped to define the areas beneath. Its chunky staircase splits the room in two, separating the kitchen and bathroom on one side from the living room and office on the other.

Mezzanines, of course, are only effective if you have high ceilings to play with. Even here, although there is plenty of room underneath the structure, space above is tight. Sitting up in bed is possible; standing, more difficult, unless the giant skylight, installed right above the bed, is open. Operated by remote control, this huge window allows light to flood into the interior and also provides a gateway to Hills's tiny roof terrace beyond. There's another bonus to this feature, too. By creating a see-through ceiling to the bedroom (with views of sky and stars, of course), the designers cleverly avoided any claustrophobia that might have come from sleeping in such a shallow space. (Blackout and heat-diffusing blinds mean Hills can control temperature and light.)

Beneath the mezzanine is the office, a neat row of 'floating' white units topped with a reclaimed mahogany worktop. This continues beyond the units to form an integral desk at one end, so Hills has no need for any extraneous furniture. The work station includes everything you could ask for: built-in wall lights (again, no need for clutter-inducing free-standing lamps); copious amounts of storage space; a built-in (but shut away) lightbox. There is even space for a state-of-the-art plasma television, just in case Hills saves up enough money to buy one.

Opposite the office is the living 'room' – a giant 1970s leather sofa which curves languidly around the walls, an armchair, a cowhide rug and a smoked-glass coffee table. Defined only by the furniture, this area is flexible enough to double as a

architect Joanna Rippon. Realizing they had no chance of squeezing everything onto one floor, their first trick was to add an extra level – a mezzanine – to accommodate a sleeping area. Suspended from the ceiling, the structure is just big enough for a bed, its metal frame cleverly doubling as the bed surround. Adding a mezzanine was an ingenious solution to

OPPOSITE Above the mezzanine bed deck, the designers installed a giant skylight. This provides access to Hills's tiny rooftop terrace and makes the shallow sleeping space seem less claustrophobic, as well as lighting the whole interior.

THIS PAGE Brilliantly neat and compact, the office is tucked beneath the mezzanine. It comprises, simply, a row of units topped with reclaimed mahogany.

meeting room when Hills sees clients and provides plenty of seating for parties.

At the other end of the room is the kitchen and a small bathroom which is tucked (almost invisibly) behind a white door. The kitchen, which – after all – takes up virtually half of the floor space, feels capacious with its line of white units and semi-see-through furniture. The tour de force here, however, is the amount of ingenious built-in storage, cleverly designed so that you don't even realize it's there. The fridge and the microwave are concealed within the mezzanine staircase (only their doors are visible from the kitchen), and all the other kitchen goods (washing machine, dishwasher, rubbish bin) are hidden within the white units, so the overall effect is one of sleek uniformity.

Built-in storage is one of the key ingredients of the successful small home because, tucked into the structure of a room, it doesn't intrude into the open space and so makes the place feel bigger and less cluttered. Here it has been exploited to the full, not only in the kitchen and office but elsewhere. A series of white floor-to-ceiling cupboards, which constitute the side 'wall' of the apartment, conceal vast amounts of clothes and clutter; cupboards in the living 'room' hide the music system, eliminating the usual mess of speakers and cables.

LEFT With its integral desk and built-in lamps, Hills's office-meeting room needs no extra furniture and provides just the right amount of storage. All is concealed inside the floating cupboard unit, so the office does not intrude into the living space (ABOVE).

BELOW By splitting the studio in two by means of the mezzanine staircase, the designers were able to give each part of the downstairs space a distinct identity without using walls.

Because Hills had so much stuff to accommodate, the designers also included some more open storage space. In the kitchen, a stainless-steel rail, which is attached to the wall along the length of the units, houses baskets of cutlery and utensils. Opposite, a shelving unit, the back of which cleverly forms the stairway wall, is filled with wine and tableware. Cantilevered off the floor (like the office units), this 'floating' piece of furniture demonstrates another canny space-enhancing trick: leaving a gap between furniture and floor, so that the flooring continues underneath, makes a space seem bigger.

Lighting (something photographer Hills was keen to get right) has also been used cleverly in this regard. Alongside the dimmable halogen spots which light the main space, tungsten tubes were tucked underneath the units and above the cupboards. While the fittings are invisible, a warm glow emanates from the edges of the furniture – an effect which is particularly striking at night and suggests there is space beyond.

With its white walls and monochrome furnishings providing the perfect simple

backdrop, this once one-dimensional space is now a fully functioning multi-purpose home. Hills has space to work, sleep, eat and entertain. 'I often have 30 people dancing here,' he admits. Lucky, then, that he has the pebble-like resin and marble floor. Hard-wearing and fantastically tactile, it was also right on brief. 'What I really wanted,' Hills explains, 'was an urban beach house.'

ABOVE LEFT Maximum storage means Hills can maintain a minimal look. A rail above the worktop holds cutlery and utensils.

ABOVE RIGHT To free up wall space, Hills opted for low, cylindrical heaters rather than conventional wall-mounted radiators.

OPPOSITE The kitchen feels light and spacious with its white units, effective lighting and semi-see-through furniture. The custom-built white cabinets hold a washing machine and dishwasher, while the fridge and microwave are tucked into cupboards within the mezzanine staircase (THIS PAGE). The tiny bathroom is tucked inside the white corner cupboard.

THIS PAGE AND OPPOSITE ABOVE The living room might be small, but it doesn't compromise on comfort. Although only 3.5 m (11½ feet) wide, it has room for two squashy sofas, a coffee table and a television. To give the impression of space, the architect's trick here was to keep the decoration of the room to a minimum (floors are stone; walls are white) and to keep all clutter out of sight (no trailing cables or piles of DVDs). The fact that the front wall is all window also makes the room seem boundariless and bigger than it really is; the outdoor space feels like an extension of the interior.

neat and narrow house

This tall, thin modernist house in London gives a brilliantly literal interpretation of living in a small space. Built on a site hardly big enough to swing a cat in and squeezed between buildings on either side, the place looks more mini office building than comfortable family home, yet the latter is just what it is. Behind its slender glass façade, the property boasts three bedrooms and three bathrooms; a kitchen, living room and conservatory; a study, a laundry room and a lobby. It's even got a roof terrace big enough to fit a table and chairs for four. All in all, plenty of room for owners Ben and Geraldine Atfield and their son, Thomas.

From the outside it is hard to believe that such a tiny building could accommodate so much, but architect Jo Hagan designed the place ingeniously. Unable to extend laterally, he built upwards instead, stacking seven small-scale levels one on top of the other. What he created, in essence, was a mini skyscraper (an apt conceit given that the City of London's high-rises are just streets away) with as much internal space as your average terraced house – quite a feat on a plot of land just big enough for a London bus. It's 3.5 m (11½ feet) wide by 10 m (33 feet) deep, to be precise.

Exploiting space vertically rather than horizontally was a canny trick (and an economical one in a city where land comes at a premium) but it did pose challenges, particularly when it came to planning the layout of the house. Whereas most homes allow an easy, same-level relationship between rooms used in connection with each other (the kitchen and the living room, for example), here lateral connection was impossible. Instead, each floor was given over to one living function (sleeping, say, or eating) and deciding which room should go where took on an altogether more crucial aspect. The Atfields, after all, didn't want to spend all their time travelling up and down between floors.

LEFT The top floor of the house, which is half conservatory and half roof terrace, has spectacular views across the city. To highlight this, a fake window in the wood-clad wall frames a section of the surrounding landscape.

LEFT Tucked into a tiny space between existing buildings, this little house could be constructed in only one direction: up. Seven storeys were stacked up to create the same amount of space that you would find in a conventional home. Unlike your average house, however, each floor accommodates just one room, with the public spaces – living room, conservatory, terrace – at the top and the private – bedrooms and bathrooms – at the bottom. The kitchen is between the two on floor three for easy access (see plan, OPPOSITE). With its glazed façade, this mini skyscraper looks quite at home in its surroundings and, though it is the antithesis of most laterally biased living spaces, it functions very effectively as a family home.

OPPOSITE Taking up the least possible space at the back of the building is a narrow staircase, but the owners use it far less than the mini elevator which runs from ground floor to top.

In the end, they reversed the usual formula of bedrooms at the top and living rooms at the bottom by placing the 'public' spaces on the fourth and fifth floors. Here the façade of the building is glazed at both front and back, which not only fills the interior with light (there are no curtains or blinds) but also gives fantastic views over the city. It made sense, then, to use this area for the living room and conservatory (which leads onto the roof terrace), where they would entertain and spend most time. The bedrooms were positioned on the first and second floors where only the front façade is glazed (and can be curtained off for privacy) and where the darker back of the house could be used for en suite bathrooms. The kitchen was placed in between (on floor three) to allow easy access from above and below.

Standing in these self-contained spaces with no views through to another room is an odd sensation, but the interior doesn't feel squashed or claustrophobic. This is largely thanks to that fully glazed façade, which – as well as turning the building into a mini modernist masterpiece – connects internal and external space so intimately. With wall-to-wall and floor-to-ceiling views at every level (bar the basement, of course), the house feels boundariless and the surrounding landscape becomes just an extension of the interior. This merging of indoor and outdoor space – typical of many modernist homes – visually tricks you into thinking the place is bigger than it is.

There are more prosaic reasons, too, why the interior feels spacious. Planning each floor of the house extremely tightly, Hagan made sure he used every bit of available space to the full. He built in wet-room bathrooms (no need for a shower cubicle) with integral shelving around the bath; he installed underfloor heating (no need for radiators); and – most important of all – he built in copious amounts of secret storage, making use of dead space that would

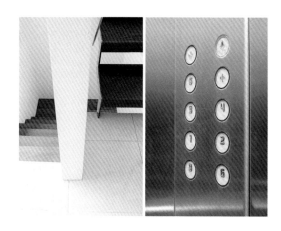

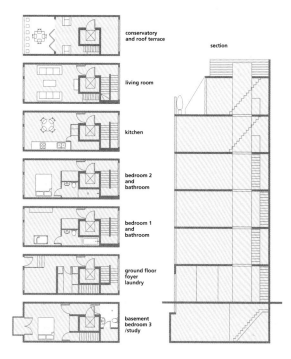

conservatory and roof terrace

section

living room

kitchen

bedroom 2 and bathroom

bedroom 1 and bathroom

ground floor foyer laundry

basement bedroom 3 /study

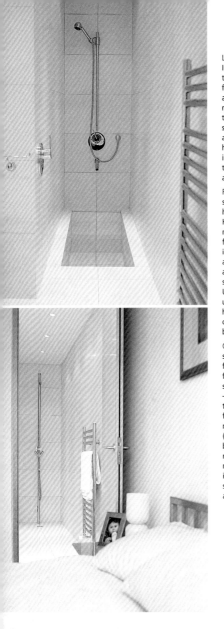

LEFT AND BELOW Ingeniously designed, the bathrooms don't feel as tiny as they really are. Built-in and wall-mounted fixtures free the central space, while secret storage areas allow clutter to be hidden from view. The integral shelf around the bath also provides a useful storage spot.

RIGHT Every bit of space in the building has been used to the full. Here, the entrance to the main bedroom has been fitted with a large built-in cupboard to accommodate clothes and clutter, thus freeing space in the room itself. Unlike the 'public' areas upstairs, the bedrooms have floor-to-ceiling curtains so that they can be screened from view.

OPPOSITE With its sleek white units, stone floors and simple modern furniture, the kitchen seems bigger than most – an effect enhanced by the window wall at the front. Although there are no eye-level cupboards (avoided by the architect because they would have made the room seem more cramped), there is just enough storage space to accommodate all the kitchen clutter.

otherwise have been wasted. At living room level, the boiler and heating paraphernalia are hidden under the stairs; in the bedrooms, capacious built-in wardrobes mark the entrance; in the bathrooms, mirrors conceal storage shelves. Even on the stairway, tucked at the back of the building to take up the least possible room, storage cupboards and lights are built into the walls.

The decoration of the house, too, does all it can to make the place feel expansive. White walls and simple stone flooring reflect the light; furniture is simple and streamlined; accessories are kept to a minimum. The result? A house that feels light, airy and spacious, despite its diminutive dimensions, and one which works brilliantly as a contemporary home.

There is one element that remains tiny, however: the lift. A life-saver in a seven-storey household, the two-man elevator cuts a swathe from the ground floor of the building right up to the top. 'We use it as a dumb waiter,' Ben Atfield laughs, 'because it's more or less the same size.'

Floor plan labels: bathroom, study/guest bedroom, kitchen, living/dining area, dressing area, bedroom, bathroom

flexible space

Making the most of your space is one of those axioms of interior decorating that we all have in mind when we think about doing up our homes. Chanted by celebrity designers on television, analysed by experts in the pages of interiors magazines and demonstrated in a host of self-help DIY design books, this little phrase is something we all know by heart. Few of us, however, have put it into practice as cleverly as the designer of this little apartment, perched on the 17th floor of a New York apartment block.

With a wraparound roof terrace on three sides, this New York apartment has fantastic views over the city – something designer David Khouri exploited by creating a series of floor-to-ceiling glass doors around the property. These not only allow light to pour into the apartment from all sides but also extend the sense of space, for the terrace itself – decorated with a pattern of tiled and planted paving and upholstered furniture – feels very much part of the interior. The step up to the terrace (ABOVE RIGHT), topped with white vinyl cushions, can double as a sitting area.

In a small space it is vital, of course, to make the most of every bit of it, something the previous owner of this property had singularly failed to do. Though the place wasn't sizeable (around 93 square metres or 1,000 square feet), it had fair credentials: a reasonable amount of floor space; windows on three sides; a sweep of roof terrace giving spectacular

THIS PAGE AND PICTURE ON PAGE 24 On one side of the apartment is the living-dining room, filled with colourful and quirky furniture all designed by Comma (except for the vintage sofa).

OPPOSITE A sleek, modern storage solution, the wall of cupboards hides everything from books and CDs to the hi-fi. Suspended off the floor and lit right around its perimeter, this unit and the polished stainless-steel box beside it seem less solid and thus don't diminish the overall sense of space.

views over the south of the city. Nothing, however, had been done to fulfil this potential. The interior, for a start, was boxy and cramped and, extraordinarily, brick walls on all sides meant that there was little sight of the roof terrace (and thus those views) from inside.

The new owners of the apartment, Avi Pemper and Mark Rabiner, knew something had to be done, but rather than going down the conventional route and calling in an interior decorator, they asked product designer David Khouri of Comma to undertake the project for them. 'They came in to see our work and bought a screen,' explains Khouri. 'Things progressed from there.' Though on the face of it this might seem a rash decision, it is easy to see why the couple were won over. Comma designs are funky, colourful and original (most of the furniture in the apartment is theirs) – just the qualities Pemper and Rabiner wanted for their new living space.

With faith in his design expertise, the couple gave a broad brief to Khouri. 'They wanted to update the apartment and to turn it into somewhere that would keep them in the city at weekends,' he explains. 'They also wanted me to keep a bit of the building's original 1950s character.' The

first thing he did, of course, was to knock out the brick wall at the front of the building and replace it with floor-to-ceiling glass doors (reinforced in strategic places). This had an immediate and dramatic effect. Not only did light now pour into the interior, but the place instantly seemed more open and expansive, something that Khouri then enhanced by taking out the existing dropped plaster ceiling.

Once the structure of the interior had been rejigged, Khouri then set about rearranging the internal layout of the space. Rabiner and Pemper, like most contemporary couples, wanted an open-plan, do-it-all living area – somewhere they could eat, entertain, listen to music. They also wanted bathrooms, a kitchen, two bedrooms, a dressing room, a den and an office. Rather than splitting the interior up into boxy rooms, however, Khouri decided instead to create flexible space. On one side of the apartment, he established a living-dining room (separating the two areas simply with that signature orange screen) and on the other, he constructed a series of three rooms – a master bedroom, a dressing room (just two storage units with a passage in between) and an office-den which can be turned, in an instant, into another bedroom.

Separated only by sliding partitions ('in a small space, it's nice not to have to deal with doors,' says Khouri), these three rooms can be left open to each other to create one airy bedroom wing or enclosed to create private space – particularly useful when the couple have guests. Shut off from the dressing room, the combined office-bedroom with its little adjacent bathroom can thus be transformed into a self-contained suite.

The bathrooms and the kitchen could not be reworked structurally but Khouri did all he could decoratively to make the best of them. He mirrored the ceiling of

THIS PICTURE Separated by sliding doors, the bedroom, dressing area and office can be left open to each other to create one giant sleeping space or enclosed for privacy. The office (in the foreground and INSET) can also be turned into a spare bedroom; the grey chairs (below) unfold to make a queen-size mattress.

BELOW With plenty of storage in the two large units in the dressing area, the bedroom can be kept uncluttered. Though minimally furnished, it isn't stark. The grasscloth wallpaper (seen in main picture) and resin floor give textural interest.

the units and worktop; orange for the sink), and the walls are lined with cupboards moulded from self-skinning urethane (the stuff used to make dashboards). And that's not all. Hidden both above and beneath the cabinets are three different colours of neon, so that the room can change colour at the flick of a switch ('the couple wanted party lighting,' Khouri explains).

With his innovative designs and clever use of materials Khouri has given the apartment a cool and individual stamp, but there is more to the place than mere designer looks; it is also full of pragmatic solutions for small-space living. For a start, the apartment is full of storage. The dressing room has two giant wood-veneered units; the bathrooms, stacks of secret space for stashing bathing kit; the kitchen, units galore. And then there is the living 'room' with its funky storage wall. Topped with rosewood and lined in red plastic laminate, this accommodates all manner of bits and pieces and even houses a little bar at one end. Large and solid, this iconic piece could intrude on the rest of the space had Khouri not suspended it off the floor and sunk lighting around the perimeter to make it 'float' (another natty space-saving trick).

Finally, there's the floor. A uniform plane throughout the apartment, it is made of glossy apoxy resin in a light cobalt blue. 'We wanted it to look like a swimming pool,' explains Khouri, 'so we gave the manufacturer a colour chip to match.' As well as being extremely hard-wearing, bringing all the disparate bits of the apartment together and giving the place a hint of 1950s colour, this shiny, highly reflective surface makes all the furniture seem to float (that swimming pool conceit worked like a dream) and fools the eye into thinking the apartment is far bigger than it really is. The original owner wouldn't recognize the place.

the main bathroom to double the space visually and clad the walls of both in brilliantly reflective white structural glass. Unwilling to make do with average fixtures and fittings, Khouri had a bath and basin made out of white Corian (by Wilsonart Corporation) and supplemented these with bespoke plastic and designer pieces (the long rectangular Cappellini sink in the master bathroom is one of these).

The kitchen, too, is the antithesis of average. Though it is a tiny space, it has bags of impact because of its ingenious and original design. All the surfaces are faced in a Corian-like material (white for

ABOVE Though tiny, the kitchen manages to be both funky and functional. With wraparound white units at floor level and moulded urethane cupboards at eye level, there is plenty of storage. The appliances are built in and the hob set into the worktop to make the most of the space.

THIS PAGE The two bathrooms may be small but they feel bright and spacious because of Khouri's clever use of materials. Walls are clad in highly reflective white structural glass; fittings are white and in the master bath the ceiling is mirrored to double the space visually.

escape from the loft

Not many of us, I would hazard to guess, would choose to move from an expansive loft space into a teeny weeny terraced house, but interior designer Helen Ellery did just that. She had had enough of that trendy open-plan lifestyle, of multi-purpose living zones and all that undemarcated space. What she craved, instead, were some good old-fashioned rooms. 'In a loft, you have just one big area to work with,' she explains. 'I wanted to have a number of different spaces so that I could stamp a distinctive personality onto each.' She also wanted somewhere that would accommodate both her work and her living space without the one intruding on the other (something that is particularly tricky to achieve in a one-floor, open-plan loft).

This tiny little Georgian property on a quiet London street seemed, then, an unlikely place for Ellery to realize her ambitions. Though built on three floors, with a converted basement, the house is very small (the photographs are deceptive), and what's more, when she bought it there were no rooms to speak of. The building had served a series of different functions over the centuries (hosiery store, tripe merchant and salvage yard to name but three) and its original internal structure had been stripped out years previously. What Ellery inherited was, essentially, a shell, and a miniature one at that.

Ellery, however, saw the potential of the place and was particularly drawn by the fact that she could create a categoric split between her home and her office by placing them on different floors (her business, The Plot, now occupies the basement and ground floor; her home, the top two floors). The size of the building also worked in Ellery's favour. Disenchanted with loft living, she wanted her new home to be more cosy country cottage than minimal urban penthouse. Diminutive dimensions were thus a bonus even though space would be tight.

Having only a small area to work with, Ellery planned the layout of her home very

OPPOSITE AND ABOVE RIGHT Interior designer Helen Ellery let neither size nor location cramp her style when it came to doing up her diminutive London home. The living room looks more country cottage than urban terrace and, though tiny, is filled with largish pieces of furniture. The expansive glass-topped cabinet and shelves hung in the alcoves beside the fireplace provide useful storage space.

BELOW RIGHT Ellery decided to use the basement and ground floor of the house for her office, keeping the top two floors for her home. On the first floor is the living room, dining room and kitchen (with a roof terrace outside); on the second, two bedrooms and a tiny bathroom. The staircase is carpeted with a grass green runner – something which, along with other rugs in varying natural greens, helps to bring a touch of the countryside to this inner city location.

BELOW Ellery's kitchen on the first floor doesn't feel cramped because it is left open to both the dining and living areas. To avoid these areas merging into each other decoratively, Ellery gave each a distinct identity. The kitchen is defined by a floor of black-and-white mini tiles and by a row of shiny black units.

carefully. On the lower floor, she needed to accommodate a living room, dining area and kitchen (quite a challenge in such a restricted space). Rather than slicing the interior into three self-contained rooms, Ellery created just one solid partition, a wall which runs across half the space and cleverly defines three separate areas. At the front of the house is the living room which, semi-enclosed by the central wall, feels private and cosy. Tucked behind

the wall at the back of the house is the kitchen. In the space between, at the top of the stairs, is the tiny dining area, its perimeter defined only by a change of flooring and a giant stainless-steel fridge.

Although all three 'rooms' are open to the others (a trick which, cleverly, makes them seem bigger than they really are), each has its own distinct identity. The living room is clubby and traditional with its chunky check sofa, large wooden cabinet and raw brick fireplace. The kitchen is rustic and chic, a combination of sleek black units ('almost invisible when the sun shines on them'), dark wood worktops and rails of shiny steel utensils. The most striking feature here, however, is the floor, which has been covered with black-and-white mini tiles – a device that divides the kitchen visually from the dining area and also gives it a grandeur which belies its size. 'It's a mickey-take on those floors you find in stately homes,' laughs Ellery. The dining 'room'– the smallest of the three – comprises a simple wooden table and four chairs positioned underneath a giant old railway clock.

Convention dictates that a small space should be furnished with small pieces of furniture but Ellery has turned that on its head, filling her home with unexpectedly large-scale items: the giant fridge, the wall-to-wall sitting room cabinet, the oversized clock. 'It's a myth that you can't use big things in small spaces,' exclaims Ellery. 'Furnishing with oversized objects – as long as they don't stop you moving around freely – makes the atmosphere seem bigger.' There is no doubt that these pieces do appear to stretch the space around them; they also give a quirky *Alice in Wonderland* feel to the interior (the black-and-white miniature tiles do the same), which adds an extra, highly individual dimension.

Upstairs, too, Ellery used this little and large conceit. In her bedroom at the front

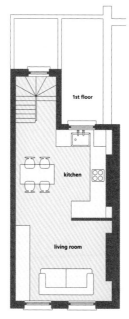

1st floor

kitchen

living room

2nd floor

bathroom

bedroom

bedroom

LEFT Ellery extended the bedrooms into the loft to make them roomier and squeezed a bathroom onto the landing.

of the house, the stripped sash windows are dressed with oversized pelmets (valances) and curtains in overblown floral fabric, which make the room feel larger than it is – a canny trick given that it's actually fairly small. Aside from one large built-in storage unit, there is only room for a bed (albeit a shapely, vintage, wooden one), a small side table and an old working range, which was originally installed in the kitchen.

Fitting two bedrooms and a bathroom into the tiny upstairs floor was no easy feat, but Ellery made use of every available space. She took out the existing ceilings and extended the bedrooms up into what would have been the loft, giving them more room and also a more shapely, pitched outline. She then squeezed a narrow bathroom onto the landing which, otherwise, would have been

TOP LEFT Quirky elements give the interior a contemporary, highly personal stamp. An upside-down cup and saucer becomes a lampshade, while a giant railway clock brings an *Alice in Wonderland* sense of scale to the dining area (CENTRE).

CENTRE LEFT The house looks rustic and cosy with its tongue-and-groove panelling, chintzy colours and comfy furniture, but it is not a country cottage pastiche.

BELOW LEFT Stacks of storage, from shelves and plate racks to hanging rails and hooks, keeps the kitchen neat.

wasted space – a good solution in any small house. Because the room is so tiny, Ellery had to get the fittings especially made but she didn't compromise on style (cistern, basin and shower kit are miniature versions of grand traditional pieces). There are other space-saving tricks at play here, too: the radiator (also a heated towel rail) is wall-hung to free up the floor and an integral shelf has been built into the tiles to store bathroom clutter.

Storage, of course, is key in a space like this, and Ellery has plenty. The tiny spare bedroom has a platform bed (accessed by an old wooden ladder) with capacious cupboards underneath. The main bedroom has a large wardrobe and built-in alcoves for sweaters and shoes. In the living room, there is the long, glass-fronted cupboard; in the kitchen, old-fashioned plate racks, hanging rails and shelves.

None of the above, however, feels intrusive, because Ellery's decorative scheme unifies every bit of the interior. Not only has she used a limited palette of soft country colours (duck-egg blues and rich creams) throughout the house, she has

RIGHT AND OPPOSITE Storage is the key to living successfully in any small space. In the master bedroom Ellery installed a large built-in wardrobe (in tongue-and-groove to match the walls) and a unit of open storage boxes to house her clothes. With its duck-egg-blue walls, old-fashioned furniture and floral curtains, this room feels far removed from the urban landscape outside.

BELOW LEFT AND RIGHT Ellery used the dead space on the landing to accommodate this tiny bathroom, and even here she didn't compromise on style. She had grand, traditional fixtures made to fit and incorporated a built-in shelf beneath the mirror for her perennial displays of flowers. The towel rail was wall mounted to free floor space.

also reinstated the tongue-and-groove panelling which would originally have lined the walls. Rather than making the place seem smaller – a result you might expect from such a linear feature – it looks completely at home and gives the interior a cohesion and rustic charm.

Ellery's home is no country cottage pastiche, however: off-beat touches bring the interior bang up to date. There are the contemporary paintings by Robert Clarke, for example (floral, of course). There are the carpets, rugs and runners in varying natural greens (rapeseed; country lawn; fields of wheat and so on). There is the brown felt kitchen blind that looks for all the world like a roll of turf. And there is real nature, too. Vases and jugs filled with blossoms. Cedar window boxes planted with wild flowers. The roof terrace covered with pots of plants and herbs. With outdoors as tangible as this, this dwelling feels rural and boundariless – quite an achievement for a tiny city terrace.

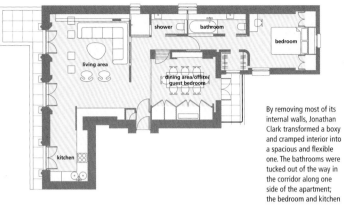

(BOTTOM LEFT) placed at either end; and the biggest, central space turned into a giant living-dining area (OPPOSITE, BELOW LEFT AND BELOW RIGHT). With natural light pouring in from three sides, this room is bright, gallery-like and adaptable. Furnished simply with streamlined and modular pieces, such as a simple corner sofa and a sleek bench-shelf, it works both as a social space and as a more intimate family living room.

By removing most of its internal walls, Jonathan Clark transformed a boxy and cramped interior into a spacious and flexible one. The bathrooms were tucked out of the way in the corridor along one side of the apartment; the bedroom and kitchen

classic convertible

Now, as you know, this is a book about small spaces. So how can we, I hear you cry, include an apartment that is so palpably large? Well, the thing is, it's not; it just appears to be. At 86 square metres (925 square feet), this first-floor apartment is no bigger than a smallish basement flat, but with its high ceilings, ingenious layout and clever design, it looks – of course – twice that size.

Home to Rashna Mody-Clark, art director of *House & Garden* UK, and architect Jonathan Clark, the place did not always seem so expansive. When they first bought it, the interior was a tangle of partitions and boxy rooms with one long, dark, curved corridor connecting the front of the house to the back. 'It had been converted badly in the 1980s,' explains Clark, 'and it was a very divided space. Rashna hated it.' Clark, however – drawn by the height and by the volume of the place – knew he could do something with it.

The property had other noticeable assets, too. For a start, it was end of terrace,

which meant natural light could pour in on three sides. And then there was the fact that it borrowed space from the next-door building. Not only is the communal staircase situated in the adjacent house but – bizarrely – the kitchen is, too (although not obvious inside the flat, on the plan it is easy to see that the room extends through the party wall). Whatever the reason for this unusual layout, it meant

that there was a reasonable amount of unadulterated space for Clark to play with.

Once he had stripped out all the unnecessary partitions (and there were many), Clark's first plan was to turn what had been a poky three-bedroom flat into a capacious and open one-bedroom apartment. A local estate agent advised him, however, that this would be a foolish move, making the place harder to sell in

The dining area (see plan on previous page) can be sectioned off behind an ingenious sliding partition (RIGHT, ABOVE AND BELOW) to create an extra, enclosed room. When not in use this ceiling-hung divider folds away unobtrusively into the architecture of the interior; when in use, it is as solid and soundproof as a proper wall. Decorated simply and flexibly, this extra room swaps roles seamlessly, changing from dining area to guest bedroom to quiet home office with the minimum of fuss. On one side, the room is lined with white floor-to-ceiling cupboards which accommodate all the necessary kit (a folding bed and bedding, for example) and which also conceal the mini work station (FAR RIGHT). When the room is not shut off, it becomes an extension of the main living place (OPPOSITE) and home to a long dining table and chairs (FAR RIGHT ABOVE).

the future, so Clark, instead, came up with the idea of creating a multi-purpose space. Using the large, light area at the front of the house for a living room and keeping the main bedroom at the back, he converted what had been the second bedroom in the centre of the apartment into a dining room-office-guest room.

Multi-purpose rooms provide an ingenious solution to the shortage of space

problem as long as they can perform each function required of them effectively and as long as one role doesn't submerge the others (it's no good combining an office and a guest room if you allow business clutter to swamp the latter). Here the central zone is neutral enough to be very adaptable and, on account of its ingenious design, it can easily play one role (as dining room, say) without the others intruding.

Clark has made clever use of frosted glass partitions to screen private areas while bringing light into the central space. Here a floor-to-ceiling glass panel hides the shower room from view, while a shorter frosted screen encloses the corner of the sitting area, separating it from the bathroom corridor but leaving a narrow window to allow a view through the apartment.

In dining mode, this flexible space has all the requisite pieces: table; chairs; floor-to-ceiling cupboards; and a decorative walnut panel on the wall in place of a painting. It is open to the living area, creating one large L-shaped room which is brilliant for entertaining. When guests come to stay, however, everything changes. A folding bed comes out of the cupboards; the wooden panel becomes a headboard; table and chairs are moved into the living area and – best of all – the room is completely enclosed behind a sliding acoustic wall (an idea that Clark picked up from a conference hall). This substantial, three-panelled device, stacked neatly away into an alcove when not in use, is hung from tracks in the ceiling and creates a solid, soundproof barrier when extended. The soundproofing is also very useful when Rashna wants to use the room as an office (her business and computer equipment is, like the bed, cleverly concealed in one of the capacious white cupboards).

Building flexibility into an interior is a forte of Clark's and convertible design is evident everywhere you turn in this apartment. The main bedroom and bathroom at the back of the house, for

example, can be closed off from the rest of the space by means of a pivoting door (something that is particularly key for privacy as the bath is open to view from the corridor). The shower room, too, can be concealed behind a sliding door or left open to the main space to increase the light.

These twin, mosaic-tiled bathing spaces make brilliant use of a narrow strip of space on one side of the apartment (something that Clark couldn't change because of three immovable service pipes, which were fitted in the 1980s). Though you might expect any corridor-based room to be dark and poky, these

By placing the bathroom and shower room end to end at one side of the apartment, Clark maximized space for the central living area. Enclosed behind sliding doors (far more space-saving than hinged ones) or simply left open to the corridor, these tiny utility spaces take up little room but are highly functional. Storage space, for example, is hidden beneath the colourful mosaic countertops.

The result of Clark's reworking of the apartment's interior is dramatic. The place feels huge because you can see (when the doors are open, that is) right across it from all sides and also because the windows and vertical planes of architecture take the eye right up to those high ceilings. It is not only the structure of the thing, however, that makes the interior seem spacious; it is also the fact that it is simply furnished and fairly empty. Aside from a few well-chosen bits of mid-century furniture, a sofa that makes a perfect fit around one corner of the living room ('I designed the walls around it,' laughs Clark) and a few built-in pieces, there is little else. No boxes, no books (on show, at least): no clutter.

The reason for this? That good old space-saver, storage, something there is stacks of in this interior. As well as the floor-to-ceiling cupboards in the dining-guest room and the streamlined bespoke cabinet in the sitting room, Clark provided a huge amount of less visible storage space. In the bedroom, the sleek wood-panelled wall is all cupboards; in the bathrooms, the blue mosaic hides space for stashing bathing things. Most dramatic of all are the two storage 'platforms' that Clark created to make the most of the high ceilings. With one running between the dining room and bathrooms and the other from the bedroom above the walk-in wardrobe (previously bedroom number three), these mezzanine-like storage spaces are big enough to sleep on and house everything from the heating system to a library of old magazines.

'It is rare, particularly in cities, to be able to build new,' comments Clark. 'You tend to have to mess around with an existing structure and I always try to make an interior seem bigger than it really is. You have to make the most of what you have.' With every inch of space exploited to the maximum, there is no doubt that here he has done just that.

are quite the reverse. Placed end-to-end and fitted with sliding doors and frosted glass and mirrors in strategic places, they seem spacious and are filled with light. 'You have to make the best you can of daylight,' says Clark, whose use, here, of frosted glass panels to divide space (most noticeably between the shower room and the living area) maximizes absolutely any natural light there is.

OPPOSITE Streamlined and hotel-like, the master bathroom (beside the bedroom) has been left partially open to the corridor. This not only extends the boundaries of the room, making it feel bigger, but also provides an intimate en suite connection with the bedroom. Although doors are not Clark's favourite feature, he did install a swing door between this bathroom and the rest of the apartment. When it is open, there is a view across the main space from front to back, but when it's shut, bedroom and bathroom are private.

THIS PAGE Encased in American black walnut, the bedroom is the height of contemporary chic but none the less practical for that. The wooden wall behind the bed, which stretches to the ceiling, conceals stacks of storage. Though the sleek façade is marked out in regular squares, the cupboards come in various sizes: one square for small things, several for the wardrobe. Boxing in the head of the bed meant Clark could use the cupboard sides for bedside lights. The window, with its pull-up blind to give privacy without shutting out the sky, acts as a headboard.

ABOVE Shah created a small hall to hide the bedroom from the entrance. The door at the base of the cupboard is for the cat.

LEFT With an abundance of natural light and a colour scheme of warm neutrals, the sitting area feels bright, comfortable and expansive. This is also due to the fact that it borrows space from the adjacent dining area. The two 'rooms' are divided by a dark wooden desk.

manhattan
miniature

Planning the layout of a small space is like doing a complicated 3-D jigsaw puzzle and can seem just as impossible a task at the outset. You need to fit in all the requisite rooms… and you only have 60 square metres (650 square feet) to do it in. Where do you start? This was the challenge facing New York designer Shamir Shah when he embarked on the renovation of this tiny apartment on the ground floor of a classic Manhattan brownstone.

When he first saw the property, it was a mess. The kitchen and bathroom fittings were 'horribly dull'; ceilings were low and space was cramped. 'I wanted to make it clean, comfortable and uncluttered,' explains Shah. Given the size of the place, he had his work cut out.

Shah, however, wasn't daunted. He has made a name for himself designing chic hotels and shops (including one for potter Jonathan Adler), and he created a loft for Ian Schrager, the man behind a string of hip hotels. Reconfiguring this space was a challenge, but one Shah was ready for. 'Working small spaces takes more thought and careful planning,' he says, 'but it's also extremely rewarding.'

His first task was to gut the place and then to change its structure so every bit of the space could be used to its full potential. He removed the existing false ceiling and reinstated the house's original 4 metre (12 foot) one; he made the doorways taller and fitted long vertical casement windows which would draw attention to the height of the space. He then rejigged the layout of the apartment, creating a small entry hall (see above) which allowed him to separate off the bedroom on the other side and also to incorporate a wall of storage.

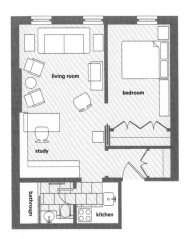

ABOVE Shah arranged the interior to give most space to the area where he spends most time.

RIGHT Often in a small home, rooms are kept minimally furnished and surfaces uncluttered to make them feel spacious. Shah chose to fill his space with a personal mix of furniture and objects which give it comfort and character. The look – sort of 1940s French meets tribal – is unfussy, and the furniture streamlined and elegant, so the room does not seem overwhelmed.

OPPOSITE Half of the living area acts as both dining and work room. The walls are lined with bespoke mahogany cupboards and shelves, holding everything from pictures to the fridge. The dining table-desk slots under the bottom shelf to save space.

Most of the apartment's floor area was then given over to a multi-purpose living, dining and working room, with a sitting area at the front (by the windows) and an office-eating area at the back. These two different 'zones' are separated only by a neat wooden desk/dining table, which juts out across the room in the centre, so – kept more or less open-plan – each seems to gain space from the other. Though two parts of the same room, these areas have distinct identities because Shah has decorated them very differently. The sitting area is all neutral colours and soft furnishings; the dining and working area is dark and geometric, its walls lined with storage units in richest mahogany.

Opting for such a dark wood in such a small space is unusual (received decorating wisdom tells us that light colours make a room look bigger), but Shah is unrepentant. 'Dark wood works better with my designs,' he explains, adding that it also contributes to the beautiful diffused light of the space. Using contrasting tones is also a clever way of dividing the room visually, leading the eye from the functional eating area to the

LEFT Squeezed into the tiniest space possible, the fitted kitchen couldn't be more compact.

soft, pale relaxing area beyond. What's more, although both bits of the room are more or less the same size, the colour change means the latter does look larger.

The dark mahogany cupboards – which line the dining 'room' walls like kitchen units – do more than provide contrast, however. Designed by Shah (like most of the furniture in the apartment), they are an integral part of the overall storage scheme, housing everything from stereo equipment, books and files to the linen cupboard and even the fridge. 'It's the best use of space in the whole apartment,' says Shah, largely because it means that surfaces can be kept clean and uncluttered. The fact that the entire place – even the bathroom – was also wired for sound ('a must in any small space,' urges Shah) makes the minimal look easier to achieve, of course.

Elsewhere, there is more storage space. In the bedroom, a large floor-to-ceiling cupboard and a custom-made mahogany chest of drawers accommodate copious amounts of clothes and clutter; in the hall, a tall, thin closet houses coats and, more surprisingly, the cat box (hence the cut-out square at the bottom of the door). 'Putting it here seemed obvious to me,' explains Shah, 'but it has raised an eyebrow or two!'

ABOVE AND OPPOSITE Even in the small bedroom which leads off the main space, there is room for modern and tribal art. There is also storage, with a wall of cupboards on one side and a chest of drawers (with space for books at the bottom) by the bed. The television is wall mounted to free floor space; a tall mirror makes the room feel bigger still.

More unusual, however, are the size and location of the kitchen and bathroom. Squeezed side by side into a minuscule space at the back of the apartment, these two functional rooms are so small you hardly realize they are there. Now, while this layout might not suit a keen cook or a sybarite, it proved the ideal solution here. By sacrificing space in the utility areas, Shah was able to give a sense of scale to the main living spaces – the bedroom, the sitting room and the dining room-office. The result? A compact apartment that doesn't feel claustrophobic or squashed, but quite the reverse. 'It is a very functional, comfortable place,' says Shah. 'It never feels horribly cramped for space.'

barbican bachelor pad

When it was first built in the late 1960s and early 1970s, the Barbican – London's experimental housing and cultural development – was in the hinterland of the city. For most, it seemed an inhospitable place in an inhospitable location. How times have changed. Today, the Barbican is at the epicentre of fashionable London, with trendy Clerkenwell to the west and even trendier Hoxton just a skip away to the east. It's become one of the city's hottest properties; an aspirational address if ever there was one.

There is, however, still a problem. The Barbican apartments (and there are around 2,000 of them) are – like many such purpose-built properties – jolly small (apart from the most expensive penthouses, that is). The originals have all the necessary accoutrements (bedroom, bathroom, kitchen, living room); they may even have a view; but with today's passion for the open-plan, some of the smaller apartments can feel rather boxy now. This apartment,

RIGHT By stripping out internal walls, Daly opened up the interior, making it lighter and more spacious. Strategically placed mirrors also increase the sense of space.

BELOW LEFT Built in the 1960s and 1970s, London's fiercely modern Barbican holds around 2,000 apartments.

BELOW RIGHT By using panels of colour, Daly made both walls and furniture appear less solid – a trick which helps to make the space seem less confined.

OPPOSITE This ingenious storage system in the living-dining area houses books, CDs and general clutter. The doors – covered in Alpi veneer – flap either up or down for maximum flexibility.

owned by credit analyst Yuen-Wei Chew, was no exception. Constructed in an L-shape with tiny rooms running off a long, dark corridor, it wasn't really the sleek, modern pied-à-terre he was hoping for. 'It was a tiny space and very boring,' Chew explains. 'I knew I had to get someone to sort it out for me.'

You can see from the pictures that he did just that, commissioning designer Paul Daly to transform the place into the ultimate urban bachelor pad. On the face of it, Daly was an unexpected choice. Although renowned for his nightclub and restaurant work, he had never designed a domestic interior before. Chew, however, was drawn by his ideas and his creative energy. 'He had made restaurant spaces

look very exciting with his imaginative use of light and materials,' he says by way of explanation. 'I hoped he could do the same here.'

Daly's first move was to make the most of the available space by opening up the

interior as much as he could. He stripped out the walls that surrounded the kitchen to make it part of the main living area (it had previously been completely enclosed but for a serving hatch). He knocked through the toilet and bathroom to make one reasonably sized room – now done out top-to-toe in funky two-tone rubber. And he removed most of the internal doors (there were three just between the bedroom and the kitchen). 'Getting the layout right was the key to everything,' says Daly. 'I wanted to create somewhere I could wander through.'

His reworking of the structure of the interior made an enormous difference to the apartment. Now space flows freely between all areas and, wherever you stand, there are glimpses of rooms beyond (a good space-extending trick). Also, by removing the barriers between the front and the back of the apartment, Daly created a view right through the space,

ABOVE AND OPPOSITE Now open to the living space, the kitchen is light and colourful. Given definition by a change of flooring and by the large overhead lighting panel, it is compact and efficient. Appliances are concealed behind doors, and an island unit, on castors so it can be moved, provides worktop and storage space.

LEFT The custom-built modular storage system is functional and funky. It 'floats' off the floor to give the impression of continuing space below – a good way of making an interior seem larger.

ABOVE LEFT A desk, built into the storage system, makes a mini home office. The seat doubles as a dining chair.

LEFT Built in a long, thin L format, the property was an awkward shape to work with. Daly made it seem bigger by removing internal doors, creating a view through the space (see page 59). This gives outdoor views at both ends of the apartment, and doubles the natural light.

OPPOSITE A play of geometric shapes, the bedroom contains all the requisite features – bed, wardrobe, mirror – in a tight configuration. The bed floats off the floor to suggest space beneath, while the panel of Alpi veneer provides a visual link with the living room. The back wardrobe unit is fixed, but the front one, which forms the bedroom wall (BELOW), is on a track and can be pulled out into the bedroom for access.

from the main living room window to the bedroom window, which not only makes the outside very much part of the interior but also allows light to flood inside.

Daly didn't stop at structural changes, however. Wanting to enhance the feeling of openness he had created with an uncluttered, relaxing interior, he dictated every aspect of the decoration from the flooring right down to the paintings on the walls. His inspirations, he says, were healing spaces and the East and his plan, to encourage Chew to eliminate clutter and pare down his possessions. 'His taste is eclectic,' explains Daly. 'There was loads of different stuff thrown together and no cohesion. We urged him to get rid of it all.'

Chew, eager to simplify his life and lead that minimal modern existence, was compliant, partly – perhaps – because he knew that the decluttering task would be relatively easy given the enormous amount of built-in storage constructed by Daly. In the main living space, there is a 'bookshelf' which combines dark wood shelves with box units covered in decorative Alpi veneer. Attached with magnets and hinges, the front of each box swings both up and down so that you can easily change the dynamics of the piece and, what's more, you can open the doors with one hand.

The most impressive storage solution, however, comes in the form of the giant walk-in wardrobe in the bedroom – inspired by a huge filing cabinet that Daly spotted at an exhibition. Made of Jacobean stained oak, with a panel of veneer and an integral mirror, this piece accommodates Chew's

vast collection of suits as well as copious amounts of other clothes and clutter. Doubling up as the bedroom 'wall' on one side, it also stands as an iconic piece of furniture in its own right.

With its camouflage-like veneer and preponderance of browns and tans, the decoration seems more funky Pop than Zen, though there are some Eastern touches: the raked-sand effect flooring, for example; the mesmeric circular paintings on the walls (by Carol Robertson); the

simplicity of the furnishing. Much of the scheme, however, was designed with a more pragmatic goal in mind: to make the space look bigger than it really is.

One canny device was to paint the walls with panels of colour, leaving areas of plaster exposed. Daly did this partly to show off the 'beautiful, uneven' plaster but, by painting only in sections, he also managed to make the walls seem less solid and the perimeter of the apartment thus more diffuse. He also made some of the furniture 'float' by leaving a gap between the bottom of a piece and the floor (again, a good way of blurring boundaries and extending the perception of space). The bed, for example, was custom-built with a shadow gap around the base.

BELOW AND OPPOSITE Chew's vast collection of clothes needed suitable storage. Daly's solution was a double cupboard, made of two units which form an iconic block when pushed together. Inside, the cupboard is customized with hanging rails and shelves.

RIGHT The bathroom is the only enclosed room, so Daly gave himself free decorative rein. Unlike the masculine look of the rest of the apartment, this room is pure 1970s with its rounded corners and orange and beige rubber interior.

And then, of course, there is the lighting – something that Daly, as a nightclub designer, is an expert at. So often overlooked in contemporary interiors, a clever scheme can make a dramatic impact, particularly in a small, open-plan space which might otherwise lack differentiation. Here, as well as illuminating the main living space of the apartment with cutting-edge multi-directional lamps, Daly used other light features to define different areas. What remains of the original corridor, for example, is transformed with two luminescent blue lightboxes; the kitchen has three separate settings so that at night it can be given an otherworldly purple glow. 'I didn't want it to look just like a redundant utility space when it wasn't in use,' explains Daly – an understandable concern given that it is now so much part of the main living area.

The result of Daly's work is impressive. Although just like its neighbours on the outside, Chew's tiny apartment couldn't be more different within. Spacious, uncluttered and very funky (all those nightclubby lights), it's just the sleek, modern pied-à-terre he had in mind.

paris match

In the pictures, this Parisian apartment looks fairly sizeable. It's got a sitting area with a large squashy sofa. It's got a space for dining. It's got the requisite utility rooms: kitchen, bathroom, bedroom. It also has a work station and copious amounts of storage. In reality, however, this is a tiny space. Measuring just 46 square metres (500 square feet), it is also a highly unusual triangular shape: not the ideal ingredients for a comfortable contemporary home.

Architects Fabienne Couvert and Guillaume Terver took on the challenge of creating one, however, even though when they first saw the place it was very unprepossessing. Cramped and dingy, the interior had been carved up into three small rooms – a fact that did nothing to capitalize on the apartment's only asset: a series of six windows which run along the wall at the front of the property.

When they set to work on the place, the first thing Couvert and Terver did was to remove all the internal partitions, to open up the space and to expose those windows.

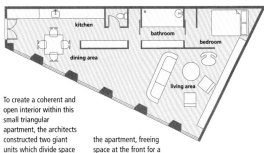

To create a coherent and open interior within this small triangular apartment, the architects constructed two giant units which divide space without confining it (ABOVE). The bedroom, bathroom and toilet are tucked behind these along the back wall of the apartment, freeing space at the front for a large living-dining area. Flooded with light from the six windows and with a view across the space from the dining zone (OPPOSITE) to the lounging zone (LEFT), this area feels much bigger than it is.

ABOVE The dining area forms part of the kitchen, which runs along the back wall. A simple row of streamlined units, this is as compact as it gets, yet a mini office has been squeezed into one of the cupboards (OPPOSITE ABOVE RIGHT).

They then had a harder task, however – to reconfigure the interior so that it could accommodate all the necessary 'rooms' without compartmentalizing it and blocking out the light.

The scheme they devised was simple but ingenious. They decided to divide the space simply by using two giant units, placed slightly apart in the middle of the apartment. Running parallel to the longest wall, these mark a separation between a row of utility rooms at the back and a living area at the front. Like vast screens,

these partition space without confining it and help to delineate the different zones of the interior.

When you enter the apartment, the first room you come to is the kitchen, which, together with the small eating area, fills one corner of the triangle. Extending into the main living space, with its perimeter defined by the dining table, the kitchen feels like a room, even though the working part of it – the units and appliances – is contained simply along the back wall under a thick ash worktop. Compact and

BELOW AND BELOW LEFT The two giant 'room' dividers provide stacks of storage. The first acts as an extra kitchen wall and is fitted with metal shelves, housing everything from glasses to provisions. The second (with a yellow interior) screens the bathroom from view, and has a wooden bench-shelf with storage space underneath.

been extended right up to the ceiling with a panel of glass, conceals the bathroom. This little mosaic-tiled room, effectively built in a corridor, has sliding doors at either end so that it can be turned into a self-contained area when in use. Although you might expect such a tiny, enclosed space to be dark or cramped, it is neither. Light from the front windows pours through the glass extension, and mirrors, fitted to the back of the dividing unit, make the most of it.

cleverly designed, the kitchen and dining area can also act as office space out of cooking and eating hours. The table becomes a desk and the white floor-to-ceiling units open up to reveal a mini work station complete with boxes of files.

The back of the kitchen is screened from the main space by the first of the giant free-standing units, which not only acts as the kitchen wall but also, fitted with a series of metal shelves and boxes, provides abundant flexible storage space. The second unit, which unlike the first has

Beyond the bathroom, at the other end of the corridor, sits the bedroom. Partially hidden from the living area by an ash screen (placed directly alongside the second unit), this room – like the kitchen – is half-open and half-contained, making it private but not claustrophobic. With little space for furniture, the bedroom contains just a simple bed and a modular storage system which runs through the bedroom opening and right across the back wall of the apartment. Here, topped with books, alarm clock and lamp, it acts as bedside table; in the adjacent sitting room, it holds everything from books and magazines to files and sweaters, allowing surfaces elsewhere to be kept clutter-free.

And so to this living-dining area. Running right across the apartment, and with its wall of windows, this space feels expansive and open – quite a feat in such a tiny place. Long diaphanous curtains, which give a good dose of colour and fluidity to what would otherwise be a monochrome and very structured space, accentuate this home's airiness and give it a grandeur that, in its new configuration, it well deserves.

OPPOSITE Along the back wall of the apartment, a modular metal shelving system accommodates books, files and pictures. While most of the shelves are left open, some are fitted with solid ash boxes which open like drawers and contain more personal possessions. This wall of storage extends into the adjoining bedroom (ABOVE).

RIGHT The tiny bathroom can be enclosed at both ends by sliding doors. On one side is a wet-room area with a shower and a tiny wall-mounted basin. The other bathroom wall – the back of the second giant unit – is fitted with a mirror and cabinet. This unit is also topped with a screen of glass, which goes right up to the ceiling to increase the sense of privacy.

the zones

living space

The place where most of us spend most of the time, the living room tends to be one of the biggest areas in a home. How often have you seen a kitchen squeezed into a corner, a dining room knocked out of existence or a side return eaten up into an interior just to make way for a large, spacious living area? It is easy to see why this part of the home demands so much space today. Where once the living room was used simply for relaxing and entertaining in – a space apart from the hustle and bustle of the dining room and kitchen – over the past twenty years, particularly, it has taken on a vast number of new roles. It is where we unwind; where we chat with our friends; where we watch television; where we listen to music. It may also be where we work and where we eat. As our homes have become more informal and less divided places, the living room has become the ultimate multi-purpose space.

It would be easy for those of us with small homes to be put off by all those giant do-it-all living areas we see in glossy magazines and to think that we simply haven't the space to create something similar in our own interiors. We should not be deterred, however.

The fact that homes are no longer expected to contain a series of single-function rooms and, instead, can contain doubled- or even tripled-up areas (the kitchen-dining-sitting room, for example) can only be a blessing for those of us with little space. We may not have a basement to convert; we may not have a dining room to knock through; but we can still create a multi-functional living area in miniature.

Of course, the more roles a room will play, the more you will need to fit into it, so tight planning and clever design are particularly crucial in a small space. In this section, I will cover the key problem areas for the living room (how to accommodate all that audio-visual kit, for example) but for more general space-saving ideas, look to the Solutions chapter.

One last thing: if you have a small self-contained living room and love it, keep it. You don't have to follow the contemporary grain by opening everything up, and there is much to be said for the diminutive, cottagey look (see pages 32–37). There are also many ways you can make even a tiny, enclosed space seem bigger (if you want to). Read on.

INCREASING SPACE: STRUCTURAL SOLUTIONS

If you need more space and have a reasonable budget to work with, think first about what changes you can

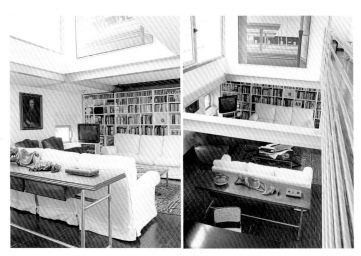

OPPOSITE The key to living in any small space is to keep it as uncluttered and unfussy as you can. The owners of this room have filled it with streamlined pieces of furniture and used a very understated decorative scheme to make it feel as spacious as possible.

RIGHT The owners of this property took a radical approach to increase their space. They completely removed the existing low ceilings to give themselves a bright, double-height living area.

make to the structure of your home. Major building projects, such as extensions, for example, will cost a lot of money, but there may be less drastic alterations you can make. Can you knock two rooms together (a front room and hall, perhaps) to create one larger living area? Do you have false ceilings that could be removed to give you more height (see page 47)? Could you incorporate the kitchen into the corner of the main living space and thus give yourself an extra room to work with? Seek advice from an architect or structural engineer before you start removing walls, but be open to the possibility of manipulating the bare bones of your home. It could make all the difference.

Consider smaller-scale structural changes, too. Even minor alterations, such as repositioning a door, can have an unexpectedly major impact. This may sound obvious, but it is something few of us think about: if a door opens into a room, it eats up a fair bit of space in the process. The solution? Simply rehang it so that it opens the other way. Alternatively, you could substitute sliding doors for swing versions or – if you're into open-plan living – eliminate the things altogether. Just think of the space you'll save. By doing away with doors you may also be able to create a view right through your interior from front to back: a great visual trick that cons the eye into thinking that it sees more space than there really is.

SPACE-SAVING HEATING
Whether you have a traditional fireplace, a gas or electric fire hung on the wall, ugly horizontal radiators or, most likely, a combination, heating paraphernalia takes up a lot of wall space – something you have all too little of in a small room. Add to this the fact that you can't, generally, put anything in front of a heat source and your scope for furnishing becomes increasingly limited. What can be done?

LEFT Radiators take up a lot of wall space, but they are less obtrusive if you build them into the structure of your home, as here. With a minimal, modern look, this heater is a graphic feature rather than an ugly inconvenience.

RIGHT Setting heating equipment back from the wall by fitting it into an alcove, as here, is also a good way of freeing space on all sides. It's tidier visually, too.

Well, the ideal solution is to get rid of the equipment altogether by installing underfloor heating, but this is not always a possibility. For a start it can cost a lot of money (though less so if you are building from scratch and don't have to take out an existing radiator system). What's more, underfloor heating isn't suitable for all living spaces and all kinds of floor covering (check before you commit to anything). The pipes and insulation which have to be laid beneath the floor also take up a fair amount of space – 8cm (3in) or so – so if yours is a very shallow room, this may not be the best solution for you.

Consider other simpler options, such as moving a radiator into a dead space (under a window, for example) or invest in space-saving heating kit. There are many products on the market designed specifically for small areas, so see which

OPPOSITE ABOVE
By opening up the ground floor of his tiny terraced house, garden designer Stephen Woodhams created a view right through the downstairs space from front to back. Because the eye is immediately drawn away from the entrance corridor and towards the open dining room and garden beyond, the place feels less confined than it is.

OPPOSITE BELOW
Simple, geometric and modern, this built-in fireplace is far less fussy than a traditional model and also incorporates neat alcoves above.

works best for you. A tall, thin vertical radiator will free up lateral wall space and, even better, draw the eye upwards, increasing the sense of height; low industrial-style spiral heaters can run along the base of a wall or, better still, be sunk into a gully; a small wood-burning stove (which will give out lots of heat) can be placed in the centre of a room or even against a window, giving you maximum flexibility elsewhere.

Solutions for fireplaces can be just as dramatic. If you are very short of space, why not take out the chimneybreast (but note that the stack will need to be supported, so again, consult a structural engineer) and use it for a storage cupboard or bookshelves? Alternatively, just simplify the fireplace by removing the surround and mantelpiece to create a plain, geometric hole in the wall. This modern solution will retain a focal point for the room (always useful), use less space and make the interior less cluttered visually.

HOW TO HIDE YOUR HI-FI

What to do with an increasing amount of audio-visual gear is a perennial problem for any home owner, but it takes on more

OPPOSITE In this pared-down apartment, the audio-visual equipment has been cleverly hidden behind a sleek panel of wood which looks more like modern art than anything functional. CDs, too, have been tucked out of sight inside a long horizontal box, which is attached to the wall like a Donald Judd installation.

LEFT With a streamlined plasma television mounted on the wall, the interior is free of bulky boxes and trailing cables.

RIGHT Even if you can't stretch to sleek units for your books and CDs, make sure to stack them up tidily. A bit of order makes the tiniest home seem more spacious.

resonance in a tiny living room. What you don't want is a collection of mismatched units stacked up in a corner with cables trailing; what you should be after, instead, is an ordered or, better still, a concealed system which will reduce clutter and thus make your room seem bigger.

If you are completely restructuring your living room, try to get as many of the brown goods as you can built in. DVD players, stereos, speakers and even the television can be hidden away in a cupboard built just for the purpose (see pages 10–17). Television cabinets may have had a bad press in the past, but the concept of concealment is a good one. It works especially well if you create not individual storage units for each item but a seamless wall of floor-to-ceiling cupboards which can accommodate all of them and more (this way, when the doors are closed, the cupboards become almost invisible). If you can't afford to build new storage, make the most of what you have and think

laterally. Place the television in that revamped fireplace – as long as the fireplace is not still in use – or put it on a pivoting arm and attach it to the wall or in an unused alcove. If money is no object, you could always buy yourself a plasma-screen television, of course, and hang it, like a painting, on the wall.

TOO MANY BOOKS

Books take up huge amounts of space, and if you want to keep a collection you will need to create an effective storage system. Hide them, if you can, in built-in cupboards, or create a shelving system (though books on show will clutter up your room visually). If you have no space for cupboards or shelves, install a long low bench-like plinth along a wall and hide your books underneath or keep most of your collection stored away (in a loft, perhaps) and just stack up your favourites on the floor like a coffee table (see page 52). For space-saving furniture ideas, see page 132.

SPACE SAVERS
FOR **LIVING ROOMS**

* Create a floor-to-ceiling wall of storage. It won't intrude on your space and it should house a great deal of clutter.

* Hide away your audio-visual kit and, if possible, hide cables under floorboards or in the skirtings (baseboards).

* Get your speakers built in so that they don't clutter up the main floor area.

* Create a heating system that works with your space rather than against it. Treat yourself to invisible underfloor heating if you can.

* Reverse the position of your door if it is taking up too much space.

* If you don't want a fireplace, use the chimneybreast for shelving or storage.

* If you do, simplify the fire surround and keep your mantelpiece tidy.

* In a shallow space, keep the seating low: floor cushions are de rigueur in stylish households.

* Invest in furniture that does two jobs at once – the stool that becomes a table, for example, or the hollow bench you can stash your magazines in – so that you need less of it.

* Keep your hoarding instinct in check; clutter is a small space's worst enemy.

cooking & eating space

In a small living space the kitchen is more often than not the smallest room there is. It may be tucked into an awkward corner at the back of a house, stuffed into a side extension or squeezed into an apartment corridor – wherever it is, it is bound to lack one thing: space. Having a small area to work with will limit you, of course (it's unlikely that you will be able to create a do-it-all living and cooking space, for example, unless you have the budget to knock down a few internal walls), but remember that a compact kitchen can be just as efficient and effective as a larger one, if not more so, if it is carefully planned and well designed. With simple units and slimline appliances, space-saving gadgets and pull-out or foldaway surfaces, you should be able to turn a tiny kitchen into a perfect mini machine for cooking.

GENERAL PRINCIPLES

If you are building a kitchen from scratch, think carefully about the shape of the room and consider what kind of design would make the most of it. Units now come in so many different sizes and shapes that it shouldn't be difficult to find what you want. Before you start planning the room, however, it is worth bearing in mind these general space-saving principles:

A fitted kitchen rather than a collection of free-standing pieces is usually the best space-efficient option in a small space.

Avoiding units at eye level, thus keeping the perimeter of the room in view, will make a kitchen seem less cramped.

Extending the flooring, the wall colouring or even the worktop of the kitchen into an adjacent space will blur its boundaries and thus make it feel larger. (This, of course, will only work if the kitchen is open, or partially open, to another room.)

Choosing wider than average cabinets will broaden the room visually (and accommodate large-scale kitchen kit into the bargain).

Using glass for a kitchen wall or ceiling is a very effective way of opening the space up (though make sure to check with a structural surveyor that this can be done before you start), particularly if the room faces a garden or a terrace.

KITCHEN LAYOUTS

There are several different ways to lay out a kitchen, so choose a format that will maximize the space you have at the same time as giving you all the utilities you need. Before you finally decide, think carefully about how you use your kitchen and pick a model that will suit the way you work.

Garden designer Stephen Woodhams opened the back of his tiny terraced house and used what had been the side return for a new kitchen. Left open to the dining area and with glass walls and a glass roof, this utility space is filled with light and seems far bigger than it really is. Storage space and appliances are all contained in an L-shaped row of dark wood units, giving a neat, sleek uniformity to the whole room.

The all-in-a-line look This is perfect for a small but long kitchen or a cooking area incorporated into another room, because it takes up just one wall (make sure you have enough room to move around comfortably in front of it). The sink and the hob can be placed at either end of the worktop (not right in the corners, otherwise you will risk banging your elbows on the wall), giving you preparation space in between; the dishwasher, refrigerator and cooker can be built in underneath. The one drawback of this kind of kitchen is that it does not offer much storage space, so you will need alternative storage areas if you have a lot of equipment (see Storage, overleaf).

The galley A row of units at either side of a room with a corridor between, the galley is a neat solution in a small kitchen. It offers a fair amount of worktop space and storage and is easy to use. If your kitchen is very narrow, it may not be practical; you need enough 'corridor' width to allow easy access to under-counter units.

The L-shape This is a good solution for a long, thin kitchen where there is not enough room for units on both sides. Place the cooker on the short part of the L, the sink, utilities and worktop on the long, and you have a format that is easy to work with.

The U-shape and beyond A kitchen with units wrapping round three or even

ABOVE AND OPPOSITE ABOVE The owner of this small studio made the most of the dead space above a communal stairwell by buying it and building in it. Installing a chic contemporary kitchen on this new 'floating' platform, she then had more space to play with in the living area. The kitchen, which is open on two sides, is compact but functional with simple units and built-in appliances.

four walls is not usually the best solution in a small space because it gives you little freedom to move in the centre of the room. If this is your only option, however, ignore the 'no units at eye level' advice and place appliances you use frequently (oven, fridge) in this higher position where access will be easier. If you can, put the dining table and chairs elsewhere so the kitchen can become just a compact machine for cooking in (see page 30).

The island Although not always a possibility in a tiny, self-contained kitchen, the island can work brilliantly if the kitchen is open to an adjacent room (indeed it can act as the room divider here – see pages 52–59). If well designed, an island unit can accommodate everything from cupboards and cooker to the kitchen rubbish bin and, with four separate sides, several people can use the thing at once without getting in each other's way. For ultimate flexibility, put the island unit on wheels so that you can move it out of the way when it is not in use (not a viable option, of course, if the island incorporates your cooker). If it is fixed, place the island on a pedestal to give a 'floating', space-enhancing effect.

LEFT AND ABOVE Even the smallest space can accommodate a kitchen. The owners of this property have chosen to incorporate a tiny utility area into their dining area rather than giving the kitchen a room of its own. Cleverly enclosed inside a floor-to-ceiling cupboard on one side of the space, the cooking area can be concealed when not in use, but opens up easily to become part of the dining area. Though small, the 'room' has all the kitchen requisites: a cooker, a sink, wall-mounted storage space, and even a microwave.

STORAGE

This is a key issue in the kitchen, where you have much to store and little space in which to do it. Start by paring down your gadget collection by giving away anything you no longer need (that old sandwich toaster, for instance) and stashing things you use irregularly (a fondue set, perhaps) in longer-term storage space (a loft or cellar, say). If you keep just the essentials, you should be able to find a home for everything, even in a tiny kitchen.

Built-in storage Get the white goods – washing machine, dishwasher, microwave and so on – built into the structure of your kitchen if possible. This way you can create a seamless row of units with everything tucked out of sight, and because nothing extraneous will intrude on the space, your kitchen will feel bigger. For a sleek and uniform finish (good for a clutter-free look), try to make sure your appliances match the rest of the units (all stainless steel, for example); if they don't, consider hiding them behind matching panels.

Secret storage There are lots of neglected storage areas in the kitchen and these come into their own when space is short. Consider, for example, concealing things in drawers behind the kick-plates at the bottom of your units (fit them with spring-loaded catches so they will open with a nudge of the foot); hide baking trays underneath the oven, cookery books in the dead space above the fridge. Use the inside of a cupboard door for a spice rack or construct a series of thin shelves within a dividing wall (as long as it is not a supporting one). The key is to not to waste even a bit of the space you have.

Stolen space If your kitchen is so small that you have no storage space at all, borrow space from the adjacent rooms. Create kitchen drawers that back, secretly, into a bedroom wardrobe, for example; extend a cupboard under the stairs;

Kitchens make huge demands on our storage space. We need shelves for tableware; cupboards for food; drawers for cutlery; racks for pans. In a small space, finding a home for all these is a challenge, but it can be done. The key is to build in as much as you can and to make the most of every bit of space. Buy specially designed corner units for awkward bits of your kitchen so you can access them easily (OPPOSITE RIGHT) or invest in extendable racks which should more than double capacity (RIGHT). Use walls or ceilings for open storage: hang racks or hooks for pans above the cooker, for example, or erect extra shelves (ABOVE).

accommodate a fridge in the dining room (see pages 46–51). Ingenious tricks like these will help you to create space and reduce clutter in the kitchen.

Wall and ceiling storage Using walls and ceilings for storage is a clever solution in any room with a small floor area. Try and buy equipment and appliances that can be fixed to the wall to free worktop and floor space (everything from radiators to ironing boards and kitchen scales can be wall-mounted), though don't go over the top or the room will look cluttered. And maximize the potential of high ceilings if you have them by fitting racks and rails on which you can hang pots, pans and utensils, or suspend modular storage units from an overhead track. One London-based couple even created a winch system for their dining table so that it could be pulled up to the ceiling when not in use.

Space-saving kitchen kit Because so many of our kitchens are small and because, today, we need to fit so much into them (dishwasher, microwaves, rice cookers et al.), there are now countless space-saving designs on the market. There

is a host of slimline and mini appliances, for example, which can be squeezed into small spaces – you can even buy a portable one-ring gas hob. There are fold-down worktops and pull-out counters; extendable corner units and expanding storage racks – all of which can be shut out of sight when not in use. There are also double-up designs, which allow two jobs to be done in one place, such as the sink that can be topped with a chopping board or the storage unit that can be turned into a kitchen table. Just a few of these ingenious gadgets will give you the flexibility to liberate your space without sacrificing all those mod cons. They won't cost the earth and may make all the difference.

Makeover tricks If you can't refit or redesign your tiny kitchen, don't despair. There are simple things that you can do to make it feel bigger. Use mirrored tiles on the splashback, for example; paint the unit doors in a reflective glossy paint (or replace them with stainless steel); illuminate areas below and above the units to give the impression of continuing space. See also Colour, Texture & Lighting, page 120.

ABOVE LEFT **In a small home, it is likely that all the appliances – even the washing machine – will end up in the kitchen. Although it may cost more at the outset, it is worth incorporating these into the structure of your kitchen (if there is room) to create a tight, uncluttered layout. Try to give the appliances the same finish as the rest of the units so that, visually, they won't stand out, for this should make the room feel sleeker and more spacious. In this minimal modern kitchen, the owners have tucked everything from the oven to the microwave behind uniform blond doors.**

SPACE SAVERS
FOR **KITCHENS & DINING ROOMS**

✱ Rationalize your kitchen kit and get rid of anything you don't use frequently.

✱ Invest in mini and slimline appliances.

✱ Create pull-out and foldaway surfaces that can be concealed when not in use.

✱ Use the walls for storage.

✱ Hang racks and rails from the ceiling for storing pots, pans and utensils.

✱ Put shelves inside as many units as you can (even the one under the sink) to give yourself twice the storage area.

✱ Use the backs of doors for spice racks or utensil storage.

✱ Put drawers at the bottom of your units (behind the kick-plates) for storing tea towels, oven gloves or baking trays.

✱ Buy a chopping board that fits over the top of the sink, making the most of dead space and hiding the mess.

✱ Make kitchen surfaces shiny and reflective to increase the sensation of space.

working space

More and more of us are working from home these days, but few of our homes have the space to accommodate an office. In a large house, the working area is often squeezed into the smallest room or the corner of a larger one. In a small house, of course, the situation is even worse, with offices shoved into tiny, cramped spaces – not places that make for a healthy and effective working environment. What can be done? The key is to create a sense of space and a comfortable atmosphere wherever your home office is sited, and to make the most of flexible office furniture and equipment. If it's well thought out, even the tiniest space can become a functional, efficient and pleasant place to work.

OPPOSITE Squeezed into an unsuitable corner or forced to share part of another room, the home office is often the room that suffers most in a tiny home. However small your work station, make it efficient with a good desk, an ergonomic chair, a suitable light and lots of storage.

THIS PAGE Exploit vertical space to the full by stacking up storage spots at the front of your desk. And wherever you place your office, try to make sure that your work is screened from view. Here a bead curtain hides the desk from the main living area.

THE TINY ONE-ROOM OFFICE
If you work in a very small room, think of ways to make it seem bigger. Do all you can to maximize daylight (install a skylight if you need to) and create an organized office system to eliminate clutter.

The desk Choose a desk that fits neatly against a wall or in a corner, or – even better – get a worktop made up to fit your space exactly. Don't waste the area underneath: use it for a filing cabinet (if it fits), boxes of books or computer equipment. Alternatively, invest in a multi-level desk which, like a terraced garden, has a number of staggered surfaces to give you a good amount of desktop storage without taking up much room.
Storage This is particularly crucial in a mini office and, whatever storage system you choose, it should be very organized so you know where everything is and can put away your work easily. Built-in cupboards provide the neatest solution because you can shut your clutter away. If you have shelves, invest in uniform box files and storage boxes (label them clearly), so that when they are lined up they will look tidy.
Computer equipment In a small space it can be hard to accommodate all the technological kit, but do your best to keep it under control. Hide the printer under the

desk or in a cupboard (internal plug sockets would be very useful here), and stack up the rest as efficiently as you can. If you have little room to move, place your monitor on a pivoting arm so that you can easily change its position.

Bits and pieces Paper, pens, diaries – the office is always full of clutter. Keep it at bay by only having out what you need and storing the rest out of sight or in a row of baskets or boxes at the back of your worktop. One neat solution for coping with messages (particularly if you haven't space for an in-tray) is to create a giant pinboard in front of your desk (filling a whole wall if necessary). Keep it organized and you should never lose anything again.

UNUSUAL LOCATIONS

If you haven't got a spare room for your home office, consider where else you could create an effective working area. If you have high ceilings and a reasonable budget,

think about constructing a mezzanine in a living room or bedroom. It needn't be big to accommodate a work station and it would give you a self-contained office. Alternatively, if you've room, you could build an extra level at the top of the stairwell or in the hall. If you have very little spare space, create a series of floor-to-ceiling cupboards against a wall and enclose your entire office – bar the chair, obviously – within it (see page 41). This way you can open it when you are working and shut it away afterwards. Similarly the 'office in a box' – something that a few ingenious suppliers are offering – allows you to access your working space as and when (and where) you need it.

SHARED SPACES

Many of us are forced to work in another room – at the end of the dining-room table, for example, or at one side of the bedroom. Doubling up a room's functions like this will be a problem if you allow one role to intrude on the other (leaving office papers all over the bedroom floor, for example), but if the arrangement of the room is planned carefully, it can work well. The office in the bedroom can be a good combination as the room's functions won't conflict (it can be one by day, the other by night), but make sure you can hide your work once you have finished for the day (if you have open shelves, screen them off at bedtime behind a partition or curtain). Good storage is essential (the floor-to-ceiling cupboards mentioned above would be perfect), and to make things easier for yourself try to incorporate flexible features into the structure of the room: a pull-down bed, perhaps, or a flap-down desk that can disappear when you need it to. If you haven't the budget for foldaway fixtures, choose furniture adaptable enough to fit both roles: a plain desk that can double up as a dressing table, for example, or a bedside table-filing cabinet.

With a worktop and row of cabinets on one side, this flexible space makes an efficient home office, but pull out the sofabed and shut away the files and it becomes a clean-lined, comfortable bedroom. To maximize this dual potential, the room has been furnished neutrally and fitted with features, such as the open box shelves, that work well in both roles. Frosted glass doors separate this room from the rest of the apartment.

SPACE SAVERS
FOR **WORK ROOMS**

* Get your office in order: nothing looks more cluttered than piles of paper.

* Create a working wall by running filing cabinets and a worktop with an integral desk along the length of a room (see pages 14–15). Even better, enclose it in a series of cupboards if you can.

* Buy uniform box files for storing your work.

* Fit plug sockets inside cupboards so you can stack up your computer kit behind closed doors.

* Don't waste space: it is amazing what you can fit under a desk.

* Create a giant pinboard for messages and memos.

* If your work station is in another room, shut it away or screen it off when it is not in use.

* Create thin drawers beneath your desk for hiding desktop clutter.

* Invest in new space-saving office designs – a multi-level desk or an office in a box, for example.

* Don't buy dull office furniture: choose pieces that would look good anywhere.

bathing space

In many small homes, bathrooms have a rough time of it. Stuffed into small, airless rooms or squeezed into awkward corners, they are not, generally speaking, the sybaritic spaces we would like them to be. Treated in the past more like a utility room than a pleasure dome, today's bathroom tends to be filled with an ill-planned medley of functional fixtures and fittings and cluttered with an increasing load of bathing 'essentials' – a particular problem to cope with in a confined space.

There are things that we can do to improve the situation, however. If you are building a bathroom from scratch or completely restructuring an old one, you can work even the tiniest space to your advantage. If you haven't a gap for a shower cubicle, create a wet room, which needs no such division. If you've no space for a standard bath, buy yourself a small one or get one built in to fit the available area exactly (see pages 18–23). Consider, too, opening the bathroom (partially, at least) to an adjacent bedroom so that it feels larger; or screening the space with frosted glass panels rather than a solid wall to increase the light.

If you have neither the budget nor the time to change your bathroom structurally, make the best of what you have. Think of new places to store all that clutter, bring in mirrors to increase the sense of space and use a few decorative tricks to make the room seem larger than it really is. Lastly, and most importantly, be strict

with your toiletries: buy only what you need and get rid of bottles, cans and tubes as soon as they are empty. If it is properly planned, cleverly finished and well managed, even the tiniest bathroom can become a sanctuary.

SPACE-SAVING BATHROOM KIT

The hard stuff If you have little space, it is a good idea to invest in smaller than average baths and basins. Tubs come in all shapes and sizes, so choose one that fits your needs or get one made to measure for an awkward space. Square or even triangular baths work well in a tight corner, but remember that they need to be deeper than average rectangular ones to give you adequate water. If you can, sink such a tub into the floor so that it doesn't take up too much vertical space.

A shower, of course, is perfect for a tiny bathroom (indeed, it might be all you can fit in). Pick a streamlined design and avoid bulky cubicles and curtains (a half wall fixed to the side of a bath makes a good screen). Choose a toilet, too, that is simply shaped and not too cumbersome. Corner and wall-mounted designs work well in a small space.

If you are feeling adventurous, seek out more esoteric space-saving bathing devices, many of which come from Japan. Quirky designs on offer include everything from toilets topped with an integrated basin (the refill water can thus be used for washing your hands) to retractable shower stalls (a circular plastic curtain descends from the ceiling to surround a central shower rod). The Japanese have even produced a 'unit bath' in which bath, basin and toilet fixtures have been ready moulded in prefabricated plastic and fibreglass. **Fixtures and fittings** Choose the simplest designs you can and get them built in wherever possible. The shower head, for example, can be sunk into the ceiling; the bath spout and taps (faucets)

Creating a mini en suite bathroom can be a good way of saving upstairs space in a one-bedroom home. Here a tiny bathroom was created without compromising sleeping space. The door is frosted glass, to give privacy without shutting out the light, and the large mirror on the back wall makes the room feel almost double its size. Borrowing space from the bedroom and kept uncluttered, it doesn't feel cramped or confined.

Showers and baths can be built into the most awkward spaces as long as you can make the plumbing work. Here a rounded unit has been created to accommodate a shower, basin and bath. Half colourful mosaic and half glass block tiles which screen the room from view but let light through, this mini bathroom fits a lot into a tiny space. There is even a soap dish attached to the glass wall in the shower.

incorporated into the wall, freeing up bath space and giving a generally less cluttered look. If the floor area is particularly tight, radiators and towel rails can be wall mounted, making the most of the dead space above the toilet, for example, or beside the bath (see page 36).

STORAGE

This is always an issue in the bathroom and if you don't address it effectively you can end up with surfaces littered with plastic bottles and toothpaste tubes – not what you want in a tiny space. The key is to incorporate as much storage space as posssible into the room so that all the clutter can be kept out of sight. If you think laterally and use every bit of the available space, this is simpler than it sounds.

In-built Built-in storage solutions have an advantage over their free-standing relations because they don't stand out or intrude into the space so much, particularly if you place them carefully. If you construct a row of wall-to-wall cabinets above the doorway, for example, it will remain hidden as you enter the room but offer plenty of space for towels and flannels (give it sliding rather than swing doors for a sleek and space-saving finish). Consider, too, building a cupboard under the basin or in the gap at the end of a bath – indeed use any available awkward space for storage.

If you haven't the room for cupboards or want something less obvious, your fixtures and fittings can include integral storage solutions. A built-in bath could have a shelf around its perimeter; a mirror, placed flush against the wall, could conceal storage space behind (if your walls are thick enough); a basin surround could hide a niche for bathroom bits and pieces (see pages 43–44). And look out for smaller space-saving designs: tiles with in-built soap dishes or toothbrush racks, for example, or a shower head with hooks

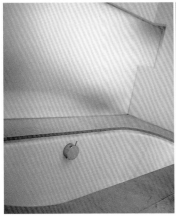

LEFT This glass screen between bedroom and bathroom can change from clear (space-enhancing) to opaque (private) at the flick of a switch.

BELOW Wet rooms make sense in a small property because they require fewer fixtures than a conventional bathroom (no need for shower cubicles, for example). Waterproofing the room at the outset, however, can be costly, so get several quotes and check your budget before you start.

for hanging bath products and shampoo. Double-up devices can make all the difference in a tiny space.

Ingenious When you are trying to maximize space in a small area, it is worth considering more unconventional storage ideas. If you have no space for a cabinet, why not erect a series of glass shelves against the window? This will give you room for bathroom bits and won't block out the light. Or how about installing a fold-down counter over the cistern (if it is low enough), or even over the bath if it is not used frequently? Perhaps it could double as a sometime bathroom seat.

DECORATIVE TRICKS

If you don't have the budget to change your bathroom structurally, or if you live in a rented space and can't make structural alterations, think of simple decorative tricks to make the room look larger. Put a giant mirror on the ceiling, for example, to double the space visually (see page 31), or – on a smaller scale – cover your splashback with mirrored tiles. And keep the surfaces shiny; the more light you can bring into the bathroom, the better.

SPACE SAVERS
FOR **BATHROOMS**

* Put a mirror on the bathroom ceiling to double the space.

* Build in your bathroom fixtures and fittings wherever possible.

* Hide all your toiletries and bathroom clutter behind closed doors.

* Use awkward spaces for storage.

* Erect a corner seat which can double up as a shelf when not in use.

* Invest in smaller than standard bathroom fixtures or get some custom-made to fit your space exactly.

* Wall mount as much as you can – radiators, cabinets, even the toilet.

* If you haven't the space for a big mirror, cover your splashback in mirrored tiles or buy a mirrored wall cabinet which does two jobs at once.

* Use reflective surfaces where you can: shiny things bring in more light.

* Avoid cumbersome shower cabinets and messy curtains: a sleek frosted glass panel will give a much cleaner result.

sleeping space

Furniture that disappears when you don't need it is ideal for any small space, and the wall bed has to be one of the best. It works particularly well in any room that has to do two jobs at once and brings maximum convertibility and value to any small home. In this diminutive basement flat, architects d-squared design created a pull-down bed which shuts away into a cupboard when not in use. With the façade a series of colourful panels (some of which provide easy-access storage), the bed is cleverly concealed.

The most personal and private part of any interior, the bedroom is a space we particularly want to get right. The bathroom may be cramped and the kitchen cluttered, but here we want a haven, somewhere tidy, tranquil and relaxing. We spend more or less half our lives in the place, after all. The good news is that turning the bedroom into a sanctuary is more easily achieved in a small home than in a large one. There is something inherently cosy about a tiny sleeping space, so if that is what you have, maximize its nest-like qualities.

Before you start, however, there are practical considerations to take into account. Where can you stash your clothes? How can you fit two beds into a space built for one? Where can you store bedlinen? Take time to resolve these issues (and you can) and you'll be on your way to creating the ultimate mini comfort zone.

BEDS
Think first about how you use the bedroom. If you are very short of space, chances are that you will need it for more than one function – for night-time sleeping and

daytime working, perhaps. If this is the case you'll want a bed that doubles up as a sofa, say, or that disappears when not in use. Equally, you may want to accommodate a spare bed for overnight guests, which can be hidden away when not required. These days there is a wealth of bedroom furniture on the market with products to suit every location and requirement, so see what is out there and choose whatever is right for you.

Bunk beds Good for kids but remember that you need a fairly high ceiling for the

person sleeping on top to be comfortable. If you are kitting out a room for just one child, consider a platform bed (just the top bunk) which incorporates a working or playing area underneath.

Sofabeds The original flexible piece of furniture, these are still a good solution if you need extra floor space during the day, or as instant guest beds. Futons are a good alternative.

Wall beds The bed that can be pulled down from the wall when needed is a brilliant solution in a tiny room, freeing floor space at other times. Several specialist companies offer an advisory service and produce a variety of designs. If you opt for one of these, however, you will need somewhere to store your duvet and pillow when the bed is shut away.

Fold-up, truckle and stacking beds
These work well as instant guest or occasional-use beds and can be hidden underneath a conventional bed when not in use. One of the best designs is the award-winning Snoozy bed by Inflate – a five-piece modular system with moulded legs that pull apart for easy storage.

Retracting beds An idiosyncratic option that you will probably need to get custom-built, these beds are winched up to the ceiling when not in use. Either crank- or electrically operated, they must be fitted to a ceiling that can withstand their weight.

MEZZANINES

If you have a studio flat with no separate bedroom or if you need to create an extra sleeping area, for example for guests or children, consider erecting a mezzanine. These gallery-like spaces make great bed decks but will only work if you have high enough ceilings to accommodate the extra level comfortably (there should be a minimum of 1.5 metres (5 feet) above the platform for it to function effectively). Get advice from a structural engineer before you embark on building and think carefully about the best place to position it. Remember that a mezzanine is an open space, so take the noise factor into account. A bed deck might look good above your living area, for example, but it will be hard to sleep if people are chatting down below.

A mezzanine bedroom will not be large, particularly if the room it is in is small, but this need not be a disadvantage. If you are very short of space, why not make the mezzanine all bed (see pages 10–17) – a sensible option as long as you have room for bedroom storage elsewhere. Buy a bed to fit if you can or construct your own, using the floor area as a bed base and simply topping it with a mattress (it is a good idea to choose a mattress slightly smaller than the base or floor, so the surround can act as a 'table' for bedside clutter – books, mugs, alarm clocks).

As well as creating an extra 'room', the mezzanine can also help to divide up the space below (particularly useful in an open-plan studio such as Guy Hills's). If it is large enough, you could use the area beneath the bed deck as an office or a more private sitting area; if not, consider using some of it for a wardrobe (walk-in, if there's space). If you have a very confined area, use a ladder to access the mezzanine level. If you have room, fit stairs and don't forget to exploit them for storage. Box steps can provide a good amount of cupboard space (indeed, they

Whether you choose a free-standing wardrobe (ABOVE LEFT) or a more ad hoc solution, such as this curtained alcove (ABOVE RIGHT), make sure you give yourself enough storage space so that all clothes and clutter can be hidden from view.

can even accommodate a wardrobe) and needn't take up too much room.

STORAGE

This is something we are nearly always short of in the bedroom. In a tiny bedroom, storage needs to be very well planned if you are to avoid clothes and clutter taking over. Consider your individual requirements (do you have to find a home for a hundred pairs of shoes, for example, or have you a giant make-up collection that won't fit anywhere else?) and then select storage solutions that will work for you. The key rule is, you always need more storage than you think.

Wardrobes The best advice is to get these built in. Much as you might hanker after an old pine cupboard or a glamorous French armoire, these free-standing closets tend to be cumbersome rather than capacious, and in a tiny bedroom they simply take up too much space. The neatest idea is to construct a seamless wall of floor-to-ceiling cupboards across the width of your room. Try painting the doors the same colour as the walls to make the unit still more invisible or, even better, give them a mirrored surface to double the space visually. You can then customize the inside to accommodate everything from dresses and suits to shoes and bedlinen. Fit shelves right at the top for stowing things you use irregularly (skiwear or hats, say); create vertical storage – at either end, perhaps – for jumpers and shoes; install a double hanging rail in one section to give you twice the suit-stashing capacity. If you haven't the time to create such a tailor-made storage system for yourself, there are companies that will do it for you. This service, of course, doesn't come cheap.

If your bedroom is too small for a wall of storage, make the best of what you have. Make an ad hoc wardrobe by fitting a hanging rail and floor-level boxes in an unused alcove and conceal your clothes

with a screen or a curtain. Create hanging space behind the bed (if you have a large bedhead), or exploit the vertical potential of a ladder for storing jumpers or even shoes.

Underbed drawers Using the dead space under the bed, these are a great option for bedroom storage. Buy underbed drawers on castors for easy access or raise the level of the bed to fit a whole series of drawers underneath. A new take on the platform bed, this will give you copious amounts of storage without intruding on the room's floor space.

Display areas In a tiny bedroom, it is unlikely that you will have room for a dressing table or even a chest, so think of other places for your photographs, jewellery box, antique hand mirror or whatever you want to have on show. Free the floor space by making the most of your walls. Fit a narrow shelf above a radiator, for example, or erect a series of box shelves (like overblown pigeonholes), which can hold things both on top and inside.

If your bedroom is reasonably long but has little space for a chest or wardrobe, erecting a wall of cupboards at one end of the room can be the best solution. Stretching from floor to ceiling, this will give you a good amount of storage but won't be as obtrusive as a free-standing piece of furniture, particularly if you paint the cupboard doors the same colour as the surrounding walls. Inside, create the storage system you need, mixing hanging rails (two deep for twice the capacity) with shelves or drawers for jumpers and shoes.

SPACE SAVERS
FOR **BEDROOMS**

* For a dual-purpose room, invest in a wall bed that can be shut away when you don't need it.

* If you have the room and the budget, erect a mezzanine platform to use as an extra bedroom.

* Pare down your collection of clothes and accessories. In a small room, there is no space to keep things you no longer use or wear.

* Use a narrow shelf or even a mantelpiece as a dressing table and top with a mirror to complete the picture.

* If you can, create a wall of floor-to-ceiling cupboards. They provide lots of surreptitious storage space.

* Take time to customize your cupboards. If everything has a place, it will be far easier to keep clutter at bay.

* Cover your cupboard doors with mirrors so that your room will look twice the size.

* If you haven't room for a bedside table, buy a bed with an integral shelf for bedtime clutter (books, clocks and so on).

* Erect a low shelf along one wall of the room (or on either side of the bed). As well as functioning as a bedside table and occasional seat, this also could house books and magazines underneath. And it won't clutter the room at eye level.

* Buy drawers that can be hidden under the bed for storing bedlinen and clothes.

outdoor connections

One of the best ways of making an interior feel more spacious is to maximize its connections with the outdoors. A view of the outside world, framed by a window or a door, draws the eye beyond the boundaries of a home and makes it, quite simply, feel bigger. The architect behind Ben and Geraldine Atfield's mini skyscraper (see pages 18–23) took this idea to an extreme by using glass for the entire façade of the house, but creating a connection on a smaller scale can work just as well. You could install floor-to-ceiling windows in a room which overlooks a garden, perhaps, or create an internal courtyard in the heart of your home. You could simply enlarge or add an extra window or two or put in a skylight. One last thing: you don't need to have a big garden to capitalize on those outdoor outlooks; views of a roof terrace, a tiny plot, an urban landscape or even someone else's garden will all help to make your interior seem larger.

By extending his tiny house with a conservatory at the back, Stephen Woodhams established a strong link between outdoor and indoor space. Divided from the main house by giant floor-to-ceiling windows and decorated with similar materials and colours, the garden feels like an extension of the dining and living areas inside and the interior feels bigger than it is.

WINDOWS AND WALLS

Just a glimpse of garden or sky will extend your perception of space and make even a tiny room feel less claustrophobic, so think about upping your quota of windows to bring the outside in. Try to create a view right through your interior if you can (see pages 52–59), as this will maximize the feeling of spaciousness and exploit whatever external space you have. If you have a roof terrace, make sure that it can be seen from inside as much as possible. Substitute glass sliding doors for walls if you can (see pages 24–31) or create a long slice of window right across the relevant wall. If you've a tiny terraced house leading onto a minute urban garden, open up the back as much as you can by creating a wall of glass or by erecting a conservatory and using that as part of your internal space. If you have built into a side return to give yourself more downstairs room (a common trick in Victorian houses), make the extension – walls and ceiling – all glass. It will give you a lot more light and make the entire ground floor seem far less confined.

If your surroundings are not particularly picturesque, use skylights rather than extra windows to give that connection with outdoors. And place them where you can see them – in a bathroom ceiling, for example, to give you views of the sky as you bathe. And consider using portholes if you have little space; they will not only give you graphic views of the outdoors, they will become an interior design feature, too.

EXTENDING THE INTERIOR

Once you have established a connection with outdoors, it is a good idea to create a decorative link between the internal and the external space, to blur the distinction between each (this is only possible if you have your own personal outdoor area – a roof terrace or a garden, of course). Creating such indoor-outdoor space is a clever way of making both house and

OPPOSITE A view can make the smallest urban home feel expansive, by drawing the eye away from the confines of the interior. Here large sash windows frame sections of a flower-covered balcony, bringing in light and a feeling of space.

ABOVE Any view of the outside world will extend the sense of space inside your home. Glimpsed through picture windows, this cityscape seems very much part of the interior.

garden feel bigger than they really are, and there are several ways of doing it. You could pick out colours from the interior to use for the garden furniture, perhaps, or match the tone of your living room wall with a flower colour. You could use similar wall finishes or even the same flooring for the house and the garden terrace.

USING GLASS INSIDE

Extend the use of glass to the interior, too. Frosted or coloured glass panels will divide up internal space effectively but seem less solid than conventional walls (and thus less intrusive) and not block the light.

MAXIMIZING
OUTDOOR CONNECTIONS

✱ Install floor-to-ceiling French windows in a room which overlooks a garden or terrace, so it becomes part of the internal space.

✱ Remove internal doors if you can, so the outdoors can be glimpsed even from the front of your home.

✱ Substitute see-through barriers for solid ones where you can. A glass roof or wall will instantly bring the outside in.

✱ If you haven't much space, install narrow windows or even a porthole to frame a section of the surrounding landscape.

✱ Maximize the sunlight: enlarge the windows and use frosted or clear glass for partitions inside.

✱ Create a decorative link between indoor and outdoor space by using the same colours or materials for both.

✱ Bring nature inside: flowers, twigs, or even a pile of pebbles will give you that outdoor connection.

✱ If your outlook isn't pretty, install a skylight instead of a window. This will bring in the light and give you unsullied outdoor views.

solutions

dividing space

In a small house or apartment, it is tempting to keep the interior as open as possible to maximize what little space there is, but this is not always the best solution. By leaving a studio apartment, for example, completely open-plan you draw attention to the fact that it is just one undifferentiated space, and it will be stuck with just one identity. If you divide it into different zones, it will instantly become more interesting and, paradoxically, seem larger. Without the perimeter of the apartment in view and with suggestions of space beyond a dividing wall or a partition, say, the eye can be conned into thinking that a place is bigger than it really is.

You don't want to divide up a tiny home into a series of boxy rooms, of course, so think of ways that you can delineate space without confining it. Instead of solid floor-to-ceiling walls, consider more partial partitions – a half wall, a sliding door or

OPPOSITE In a small home, you want to divide space without confining it, so rather than solid walls, think of more flexible and fluid solutions. Curtains, for example, can be used very effectively to separate different parts of your interior as and when you need to and they can also help to soften a stark or minimal space.

ABOVE LEFT In this dining-cooking area, the kitchen is tucked behind a neat waist-high wall, which means that the cook can chat with guests while he or she works but kitchen mess is hidden from view.

ABOVE RIGHT Use glass for fixed partitions to let the light through, as here. For something more flexible, install a sliding door or wall.

a screen, for example – or divide up your interior decoratively by using different flooring, lighting or colour in different places. This can be particularly effective in a multi-purpose room (a living-dining room, perhaps), where you may want to isolate the different parts of the room to give each definition.

If your home is already divided with walls that you can't or don't want to remove, make them seem less solid by creating an archway (square-topped unless you want that 1970s Greek restaurant look) or by knocking out holes at strategic intervals (get advice from a structural engineer to make sure the wall can take it). Internal windows can help bring light into a dark area and also, by creating a view through into an adjacent space, will help to make a room feel bigger.

STRUCTURAL DIVIDERS

Walls Solid floor-to-ceiling walls are not what you want in a small area, but waist-high or half walls can help you divide space without losing the sense of it. Place

such a partition between a kitchen and dining room, for example, and you will contain the cooking area while retaining a sweep of open space at eye level. Enclose the head of the bath with a plane of frosted glass or mosaic (make it tall enough for modesty but not up to the ceiling) and you can create an effective shower screen without the need for a space-consuming cubicle.

Materials for any such permanent partition matter, so consider your options carefully. While you may want a solid plane in the kitchen (to hide the mess), elsewhere glass or even coloured Perspex can work well and will allow light through (always useful in a small space).

For a more flexible, hi-tech solution, consider installing a sliding acoustic wall as the Mody-Clarks did (see pages 38–45). This can be hidden in an adjacent wall when not in use and will give you the luxury of closing off part of your interior when you want.

Designer Lloyd Schwan took out several internal walls in this small New York apartment, turning it into a more or less open-plan space. The biggest area is now split between a lounging zone and a dining zone (isolated on an island of carpet), with the kitchen tucked to one side (OPPOSITE). Wanting to create some separation between the eating and cooking areas, Schwan retained the dividing wall here, but carved out an internal window and a door to keep the two partially connected. With rounded corners framing pastel-coloured units, this gives a funky retro look to the place.

THIS PAGE By removing the ceilings above the living area in this Italian apartment, a previously dark and dingy space has been filled with light.

OPPOSITE In this tiny London apartment, space has been created for an office by placing the bedroom on a new mezzanine platform, accessed by a flight of steep and sculptural wooden stairs. Dividing space vertically like this is a brilliant solution anywhere the ceilings are high.

Doors If hinged doors are the enemy of the small space (they simply take up too much of it), then sliding, folding and swing doors are its best friends. Not only do they take up far less room than a conventional door, if they are well designed they should also fit neatly into the surrounding architecture when they are not in use, giving a sleek and streamlined finish.

The swing or pivoting door These work best when they do two jobs at once (i.e. by enclosing two different areas, depending on which way they are swung). See the Mody-Clark house (pages 38–45) for inspiration.

The folding or concertina door Like giant shutters, pull-out and expandable doors are perfect for dividing a large dual-purpose room as long as there is enough space to conceal the device when it is not in use. Choose a design that is easy to manipulate and not too heavy, so you won't be put off using it.

The sliding door The perfect substitute for the average door, this works wherever there is space to accommodate it (remember when not in use it will need an area of the same size or greater to rest against). Small sliding doors can usually be hung just from a track at the top; larger doors may need a floor guide, too.

Mezzanines If you have high ceilings and want to create more space, consider erecting a mezzanine. By dividing just a section of a room horizontally, a mezzanine need not intrude too much on your existing space and will give you an extra room without the need for a costly extension (see the Sleeping Space chapter, pages 96–103, for more details).

Using the floor One of the best ways of dividing space in a small home is to raise the level of the floor – but only in certain places. It might seem counterproductive to reduce the volume of a tiny room in any way, but this can be a very effective method of visually separating two areas – a dining area and sitting area, for example – and the change in level doesn't have to be great. Even 10cm (4in) or so would do the trick, though you can make it greater if you want the added benefit of underfloor storage space. It is a good idea to use different flooring for the upper and the lower areas to provide definition and also to draw attention to the level change for practical reasons. You don't want to make the two zones too different, however (it is one room after all), so think of ways to integrate the raised area into the main space, by using the same wall colouring, perhaps, or displaying similar objects.

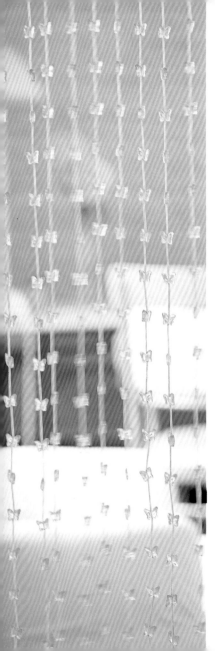

FLEXIBLE PARTITIONS

Curtains and blinds Inexpensive and relatively easy to fit, fabric drapes or blinds make good space dividers. Hung from the ceiling, they can create an instant partition between a sitting and a dining area, for example, or can be pulled down to conceal a work space when it's not in use. Blinds are the neatest solution because they generally disappear into their own fixture, but curtains can work well if they can be tidily stored (a hidden track is a good idea) and will give a softer, more fluid result. Curtains or blinds can also be used effectively to hide the clutter of an open shelving system and thus give a more streamlined look to a room.

Using the furniture Choosing furniture that can do two jobs at once is always worthwhile in a small space, and many larger pieces can make good impromptu room dividers. A bookcase, for example, works particularly well (especially if you can access the shelves from both sides), because it splits up space and provides additional storage; but many other pieces – a sofa, an island kitchen unit, a row of stools – can also create a visual partition between different areas of a room. If you are completely overhauling your interior, consider constructing a purpose-built piece of furniture that will divide space as well – a wardrobe 'wall' between two bedrooms, perhaps, or a double cupboard between the kitchen and the dining area.

Dividing with decoration If you want to keep what little space you have open-plan, but need to give definition to individual areas within it, the best solution is to divide your interior visually, by decoration. Use a different kind of flooring, for example, for the sitting zone and the eating zone; paint the walls of the work space in a different colour to those of the dining area beside it. In this way you can create the impression of 'rooms' without the need for dividing walls or partitions.

Using a fluid and flexible partition – such as this bead curtain, which separates office space from the main living area – is an effective way of dividing up space in a small house. Not only does it take up little room, it can easily be removed or tied back when it is no longer needed.

A neutral colour scheme can work well in a small home. It makes the most of the light and, if you choose warm natural colours, as here, it can add a touch of softness to an otherwise hard-edged space. Don't feel you have to stick to one shade, however. By using contrasting tones you can effectively divide up an open-plan space without the need for walls. Here, a large deep cream artwork defines the dining area.

OPPOSITE AND RIGHT
With its subtle mix of soft pastel colours and its sweep of sleek wooden floor, this interior feels very open and cohesive. The parchment tone of the walls has been picked up in the furniture and in the giant artwork, making the whole space hang together perfectly.

colour, texture & lighting

Few of us have the luxury of building our own homes or even adapting them, but we can all personalize our living spaces with decoration. This interior discipline used to be just that – disciplined – but in today's decorating world we can do whatever we like within our own four walls. Freed from the constraints and conventions of traditional interior design, we can paint our bedrooms fuchsia pink and our kitchens deep purple; we can cover our floors with stainless steel and our walls with bamboo; we can flood our bathrooms with coloured light.

Decoration is more than just self-expression, however. As well as changing the aesthetics of our interiors, it can do much to alter the dynamics of the space itself. A colour can change the mood of a room; a pattern seem to alter its proportions; and lighting, cleverly placed, can camouflage its dimensions. These pragmatic effects of decoration are particularly valuable when you are trying to make a small home seem bigger, of course, especially if your budget is limited (decorative work usually costs a fraction of the price of structural changes). So, before you decide on a decorative scheme, play around with colour, texture and pattern (sample pots and swatches come in handy here) to make sure that you are really going to make the most of your space.

COLOUR

Colour is, without doubt, the most expressive of decorating tools and often the hardest to get right. With so much choice, it can be difficult to know just which shades to choose, particularly in a small home where there is little space for mistakes. If you need some help, there are, of course, a host of well-meaning experts to consult and countless decorating principles telling you which colours should go where, but really the best advice is to browse through magazines and paint charts, choose a colour you like and try it out. Be adventurous. Many small-home owners stick to a neutral palette in the belief that pale colours will make their space seem larger (a half-truth at best), but there is room for bold colour in a small area if you use it wisely and imaginatively. A tiny room painted vivid red or deep blue, for example, will be far more striking and memorable than yet another pale cream one (remember, though, that sunlight can change colour dramatically, so that the dark red you pick out in the paint shop might turn into brilliant crimson in a sunny bedroom). One good tip is to paint the ceiling of a room a few shades darker than the walls so that, in a very tiny space, the latter won't seem oppressive and the former should seem to recede.

All white The all-white look can work well in a tiny space, for it will make the perimeter of any room disappear and, of course, it will make the most of the light. Be careful, however, to take the edge off a white interior by introducing soft and comfortable elements in the furniture or furnishings to prevent the space becoming too cold and clinical. Also, try to add some very personal pieces to the mix to stop it looking bland.

Gradations of colour Using a series of deepening colours is a good way to suggest depth of space in a tiny area and it can look very effective, too. Paint a panel of your chosen colour on a wall and then use the colours it sits next to on the paint chart (in other words, a tone lighter and a tone darker) on either side. As well as working on a small scale within one room, this can also be done on a larger scale, so that the living room, say, would be painted in the first colour, the adjacent room, in the next, and so on throughout the house. An added advantage of this technique is that by using varying tones of the same colour throughout your home, you will visually blur the internal boundaries and give a sense of cohesion to the whole space.

Introducing bold colour You can see from the first part of this book just how tempting it is to use a neutral, monochrome palette in a small space, but most of these home owners have added a dash of vivid colour to perk their interiors up a bit (those vivid green carpets in Helen Ellery's tiny urban terrace, for example). The key is to use bright colour subtly and cohesively (you don't want four clashing walls fighting for attention in a tiny room) and to intersperse bold colours with white to give each the space to breathe.

By using strong and differing tones throughout your interior you can also cleverly manipulate the sense of space, for the eye will be drawn through a doorway

or internal window if a contrasting colour (or two) can be spied through it. Glimpsing green, say, or green and purple through a yellow archway, for example, will give you a far stronger sense of the space beyond than if everything were white.

If you don't want to go for colour in the structure of your home, add it in the furnishings instead, but remember that a vivid sofa will stand out far more forcibly if its surroundings are pale.

TEXTURE AND PATTERN

Materials and finishes Colour, as we know, can have a dramatic effect on the spatial qualities of a room, but how many of us think about the role that a paint finish or a flooring material can play in the same way? We tend to choose these for looks or price alone without considering their impact on the sense of space. The thing to remember is that any reflective surface will increase the light and make a room seem larger. So opt – if you can – for the shiny and the glossy: a varnished resin floor, perhaps; stainless-steel kitchen units; gloss paint on the walls; and mirrors, well,

It is tempting to opt for a neutral palette in a small space to make the most of the light and it can work well. Don't feel you have to play too safe, however. The odd splash of brilliance, such as the vivid red lampshade and richly coloured painting here, can make a room.

wherever you can put them (the bathroom ceiling is a good place; see page 31). In this way, you can get the very structure of your home to double up your space.

Pattern Even the plainest home has pattern – the criss-cross geometry of a wall of tiles; the line of a skirting (baseboard); the ridges on a sweep of natural flooring – and in a small home it stands out far more than in a large one. Because any strong linear pattern can play havoc with our sense of perspective (think of a Bridget Riley painting), it is particularly important to make sure that whatever pattern you have works with your space rather than against it. Here are a few general rules:

• Avoid striped wallpaper: too many vertical lines will make the walls close in and make a room feel claustrophobic. If you must have stripes, go for one or two horizontals instead (though if painted right around a room, this can also have a constricting effect).

• Never let vertical lines overpower the horizontals: a long, low bench, for example, will do far more to extend a room than tall, thin bookcases.

• Don't tile a bathroom completely. The grid of the grout (or even just the joins of the tiles) will be overpowering in a small space.

• Try to create a strong diagonal focus across your interior (a change of flooring or cannily positioned furniture can help to achieve this), for this will encourage the eye to scan the longest sweep of space.

As for more superimposed decorative pattern, feel free to make it big (overblown flowers on a wallpaper, say) because, perversely, this can make a room seem larger. Use it sparingly, however (just on one wall, perhaps) or it can overcrowd a space. Small patterns can work well but, again, be subtle unless you want an itsy-bitsy cottage look. Above all, choose a pattern you like: anything can work in a small space as long as it is not overdone.

LIGHTING

Light can manipulate space more effectively than any other medium, making even a tiny area feel bigger than it really is. If your home has good natural light, make the most of it by adding windows or skylights if you need to, and by decking out your interior with reflective surfaces. If your home is on the dark side, however, don't despair. Even the brightest home needs a supplement of artificial lighting and you can just up the quota of bulbs, tubes and directional spots to suit your needs. How much light you require will depend on the weather, the time of day, the season and so on, so try to build flexibility into your system, so that you can change the mood of your lighting at the flick of a switch. And introduce a mixture of different kinds of light (cool fluorescents and warm tungstens, for example) so that you can create the atmosphere you want when you want it. These days, artificial light can do everything from replicating daylight to making your furniture 'float', meaning that even the darkest, tiniest interior can be transformed with light.

Dividing with light A good way of defining different areas within a small space without the need for physical partitions is to light them differently. If you have a combined living and dining room, for example, you could isolate the eating area with a series of downlighters (on dimmers, perhaps) and give the rest of the room a wash of warm ambient light.

Space-suggesting lighting Light can do much to increase our perception of space if it is cleverly positioned. In the past we all made do with a solitary pendant or a series of table lamps to light our rooms – downlighting solutions that could only make space seem smaller and more confining. Today, there is a vast range of light designs available, from uplighters to wall-washers, and, fitted carefully, many of

Hidden lighting can transform the sense of space in any small room, whether it is placed beneath wall-mounted furniture (OPPOSITE AND BELOW), or placed around the edges of a false ceiling to make it 'float' (BOTTOM). Here, though the source is concealed, the wall is washed with light. A glowing ball, tucked into a dark corner (RIGHT), can also transform a compact room.

them can make a room seem larger instantly. Take a look at what is on offer, get advice from the experts and pick a system that will work in your particular interior. Here are a few ideas:

• Uplighters or angled spotlights can bounce light off a wall or a ceiling, which will make these surfaces seem to open out rather than close in.

• A run of spotlights along a corridor floor (or a ceiling) will lead the eye away from the immediate environment and on into the adjacent space.

• Using hidden lighting is, perhaps, the most effective way of suggesting continuing space. A row of kitchen units or a floor-to-ceiling cupboard illuminated at top and bottom by concealed neon strips, for example, will seem to float in the pool of light and become, thus, less of a barrier (see page 17). A backlit bathroom mirror or cabinet will similarly seem to have more space behind it than it really does.

storage, display & furniture

The 21st-century home has become a refuge from the stressful and frenetic world outside and it should, the magazines tell us, be calm, comfortable and clutter-free. The image of the perfect modern interior with its sweeps of empty space is an easy one to aspire to, but it can be hard to create it for ourselves, particularly – of course – in a small home. Packed with furniture, furnishings and an ever-growing hoard of possessions (clothes, toys, bedding, tableware… need I go on?), the tiny home can easily become overrun with clutter.

There are steps you can take, however, to redress the situation. The first is to be brutal and pare down your possessions (many of us have far too much stuff anyway). The second is to buy only what you need (those fashionable must-haves will look dated in no time). The third, and most important, is to store what you have effectively so that you can keep your clutter under control, too.

Although most of us crave an ordered, well-organized living space, we don't want our homes to be regimented machines for living in. We need them, instead, to be personal, individual places, and this is where display comes in. By dealing with the mess and gaining control of our surroundings, we then have the luxury of deciding which of our possessions to show off and which to keep hidden. After all, those newly cleared counters and shelves will make perfect display space.

STORAGE

OK, so it's down to the nitty gritty. If you haven't a loft or a cellar, where can you put your winter clothes and your Wellington boots? If you have only a teeny weeny kitchen, where can you stash all your utensils and tableware? Storage is talked of as the great decluttering solution but where, in a tiny home, is there the space for it?

Well, you'd be surprised. Alongside the obvious free-standing solutions – the cupboard, the chest of drawers, the filing cabinet – there are also countless potential storage spots around the home just waiting to be exploited. Under the cooker, above the fridge, inside the stairs: such wasted and awkward spaces can be converted into ingenious built-in storage. Supplement these with the odd free-standing piece and you should find that you have far more room for putting things than you ever thought you had.

Built-in If you are building a brand-new interior, incorporate as much storage space as you can into the architecture of your home. You can never have too much. Built-in wardrobes are

Storage comes in all shapes and sizes but the main thing to remember is that you can't have too much of it. Mix and match whatever you like, from traditional cupboards (OPPOSITE) to more contemporary open shelving solutions (TOP). Piled-up clothes and clutter can look messy in a small space, so get your storage units built in if you can or, alternatively, conceal them with a screen or a simple curtain (ABOVE).

ABOVE **This fantastic Advent-calendar-like storage system has been built, unobtrusively, into a cavity along the wall so that it doesn't take up central space. Designed with various different-sized cupboards, it can accommodate all manner of bits and pieces. Also, with a mirror fitted on the wall at one side, it seems twice the size.**

ABOVE RIGHT AND CENTRE **Any dead space can be used for storage. Here, the area under a spiral staircase has been turned into a wardrobe area with a clothes rail.**

OPPOSITE **Placed on a mezzanine platform, this tiny dressing area has mirrored cupboards to make it look bigger.**

commonplace, of course, but think of other ways of introducing hiding space into the fabric of a room. Create a seamless wall of floor-to-ceiling cupboards, for example, on one side of a room. Keep the doors plain and unfussy (with push-open latches rather than handles) and, when closed, the cupboards will disappear into the structure of the space. Alternatively, create a false wall at one end of a room (or wherever you can) and use the space within for shallow shelves, or increase the thickness of a door or partition to make a narrow hiding place inside. Think, too, about exploiting dead space. Stack triangular shelves into an unused corner or build a cupboard above a doorway or underneath a basin.

Fitted storage is the least visible of all storage solutions, but don't be tempted to overdo it. Consider the proportions of a room before you start. A wall of cupboards may look sleek and streamlined, but in a very narrow room they might encroach too much on the space and a

free-standing solution may be better. Think carefully about your individual requirements and try to come up with a solution that works with your space rather than against it.

Unexpected storage If you haven't room for conventional fitted storage solutions, consider more unlikely places to conceal your clutter. Take a good look around your home and assess any wasted space. Could you squeeze a hiding place underneath the cooker or behind the bathroom mirror? Would a shallow drawer fit beneath your worktop? Consider, too, the less obvious solutions. You could raise the level of the floor, for example, in one part of your home (see Dividing Space, page 117) and use the area for stashing bulky things such as boxes of old books or ski equipment. You may be able to dig out a storage area underground (this would be ideal for a wine cellar). You could even store things inside the stairs (see page 131).

Wherever you decide to create extra storage space, think carefully about how you will use it. While the things you rarely

The best thing about getting bespoke storage built into your home is that it can be tailor-made to suit your needs. A vast clothes collection can be housed in a wall of cupboards or a mini walk-in dressing room (see page 58); books housed in shelves of just the right size (FAR LEFT); towels and bedlinen stashed away in a unit built just for the purpose (LEFT). Here a pull-out shelf has been included to make folding the laundry easier.

easier), they provide great secret stashing space for anything from shoes to box files.

The storage wall Turning an entire wall into a storage system can be a clever solution in a small home (particularly if you can use a wall that would otherwise be redundant). By providing a home for all sorts of possessions – from books and CDs to bigger items such as audio-visual kit – it will free floor space elsewhere and, contained in just one area, will give a sleek, streamlined feel to the interior. If your budget will stretch far enough, get the system custom-made so that each compartment will be a perfect fit for your possessions, and choose a combination of closed cupboards and open pigeonholes, thereby creating space for both storage and display.

For inspiration, take a look at the sleek wood-veneered storage wall in Mark Rabiner and Avi Pemper's New York apartment (pages 24–31) and Paul Daly's flexible system in the Barbican (pages 52–59).

Free-standing Although creating built-in storage makes sense in a small home, it is worth bearing in mind that it isn't a flexible solution. You won't be able to move that fitted cupboard around or take it away with you when you move house. Building fitted storage can also be a costly and lengthy process and although you will reap the benefits in the long run, this is also something that you should take into account before you start. Free-standing pieces are, by contrast, extremely adaptable: you can reposition a wardrobe; you can sell it; you can move it to a different room and you won't need to get the builders in to sort it out for you. Consider your individual situation and choose the kind of storage options that will suit you and your home. A combination of fitted and free-standing is often the best solution.

See overleaf for details on storage furniture and also see the individual chapters of The Zones for further storage ideas.

use can be stowed high up or right at the back of a cupboard, those you need regularly should be easily accessible.

Stair storage For most of us stairs do no more than lead from one floor to the next, but in a small house they can fulfil a far more significant role by providing stacks of storage space. We are all familiar with the 'cupboard under the stairs', which can be used to house anything from the Hoover to the fridge (see pages 10–17), but few of us exploit the storage potential of the steps themselves. Filled with drawers (accessed from the risers at the front) or storage boxes (accessed from the tread, which can be hinged to make things

FURNITURE

Finding furniture to fit a small home can seem a big problem. Although it is fairly easy to cut down on the incidental pieces (who needs a china cabinet anyway?), we all need some essentials, and even accommodating these can seem an impossible task in a tiny space. A table and six dining chairs may make a mini eating area look cramped and overcrowded; even an average-sized sofa may dominate a small sitting room. So, what can be done?

It is tempting, of course, to rush out and buy diminutive furniture, fixtures and fittings. Although these can work well, particularly in utility rooms like the bathroom (see page 36), kitting your interior out with mini bits and pieces is not always the best solution. A tiny armchair might fit in the corner of your living room, but may highlight its diminutive dimensions. A small-scale bed may give you room to move in the bedroom but be impractical for sleeping. The best advice is to think very carefully about what you need and to consider all the alternatives. Rather than opting for conventional furniture, for example, you could incorporate a seating or a sleeping solution into the very structure of your home (a mezzanine-bed, perhaps or a built-in shelf-bench). You could find a piece that would solve a space issue for you (a folding bed or a stool that turns into a table). You could do away with armchairs and sit on the floor. By thinking laterally and by taking a different approach to furnishing your home, you should be able to create an interior that's functional and comfortable without being stuffed with furniture.

Built-in solutions Creating fixed furniture can often be the best option in a small living space and works particularly well if you can create something that does two jobs at once. Rather than investing in armchairs, for example, run a long, low plinth along one of the living room walls. This can then act as a display shelf or a seat and also provide room for stowing books or magazines underneath. Create your own built-in bed, and you can choose to sit it on top of a series of drawers so that it offers both sleeping space and extensive storage. Built-in furniture won't be flexible in itself, but – paradoxically – it can make your interior flexible and thus get rid of the need for intrusive free-standing pieces.

Keep it low Using low, horizontal furniture will instantly make an interior seem bigger, a phenomenon that the Japanese – experts at managing small spaces – have exploited very successfully with their shallow tables, futon beds and tatami mats. By taking furniture down to floor level, you not only clear eye-level space (which in itself makes a room seem larger) but also extend the distance between yourself and the ceiling. Also, by opting for floor cushions, bean bags and low benches rather than dining or armchairs which have legs, backs and bulky bases, you will free up space and, at the same time, be at the cutting edge of contemporary living.

Multi-purpose pieces If you are investing in free-standing furniture, try to choose adaptable pieces that perform two or more functions. Pick a dining table that can double as a desk, a stool that has storage space inside, or a bookcase that can divide two different areas of a room. If your furniture is hard-working, you will – quite simply – need less of it.

OPPOSITE In a small space, invest in furniture that doubles up, like this bedhead-cabinet.

THIS PAGE Adaptable modular furniture which can be reconfigured at whim is often the best solution in a tiny home.

Storage furniture There's furniture specifically for storage, of course – wardrobes, linen chests, bookcases and so on – but other pieces, too, can be customized to house your possessions. The hollow arms of a sofa could be made to hold CDs or videos; the underside of a tabletop fitted with narrow drawers for cutlery; the bottom of a bed fitted with a storage area for blankets and sheets. With just a little lateral thinking, you can make use of the invisible dead space inside all your furniture and help keep your interior clutter-free.

Adaptable and modular Flat-pack, foldaway, stackable, extendable, adjustable, mobile – these are the kind of qualities you should be looking for when you are furnishing a tiny home. What you want is furniture that is flexible: the chair that can be brought out for a guest and then packed away again; the table that can be one height for supper and another for coffee; the bed that can be extended; the stools that can, together, form a table; the kitchen island unit that can be wheeled to one side when not in use. Versatility and convenience are where it's at.

See-through furniture In a small space you need your free-standing furniture to be as unobtrusive as possible. Choose a design that won't block the light or create too much shadow. Tables and chairs in transparent materials (glass or Perspex) work well (see Guy Hills's kitchen on page 16) and pieces made of wire mesh will dominate less than solid pieces. Best of all, of course, choose mirrored furniture for your interior. Not only will it increase the light but it will make your space seem bigger, too.

Mini and maxi Filling your tiny home with diminutive pieces of furniture will, obviously, give you more space, but don't be afraid of using the odd overscaled piece, too. A large item of furniture added to the mix – such as a vast railway clock, for example (see Helen Ellery's dining area on page 35) – can give a quirky touch to a room and also make the atmosphere bigger, conning the eye into thinking there is more space than there really is.

DISPLAY

Yes, I know you need to get rid of your clutter, but there is room for a spot of display in small homes. The key is to keep it simple – so show a small group of sculptural ceramics rather than filling your shelves with knick-knacks – and to think of ways of making your displays enlarge the perception of space.

Diminishing scale By displaying a series of objects in descending order of size you can play visual tricks with the proportion of a room or just a piece of furniture. A nest of small tables displayed in a row rather than grouped together, for example, or a series of bottles, say, lined up in diminishing size against a wall can help to make a tiny room seem larger. Experiment with your possessions and see what difference a display can make.

Tiny things A display of small things can make a big impact in a tiny space and, if chosen carefully, it needn't be twee. Line up a collection of keys on a wall, for example, or a series of tiny pictures, and you should make a graphic and eye-catching display, which (because there are multiple elements to your arrangement) will help extend the dimensions of a room.

Where to do it The main problem about arranging things in a small space is deciding where to do it, particularly if you have little free-standing furniture. Think laterally, however, and you should come up with a few potential display spots. You could prop pictures on the floor if you lack wall space, for example; use the edges of the stairs; or even hang things from the ceiling (a graphic mobile, perhaps). Wherever you decide to show off your possessions, don't overdo it. Less in a small house is very definitely more.

In a small space, the few pieces of furniture you have need to work twice as hard as normal. This funky corner sofa, for example, provides seats for the dining table and a shelf (at the back) for a telephone, and also contains huge storage drawers at one end. The 1960s-look table, which wraps itself around two curvy armchairs, also effectively saves space.

stockists in the UK

Alma Home
12–14 Greatorex Street
London E1 5NF
(020) 7377 0762
www.almahome.co.uk
Leather floor cushions.

Becker Sliding Partitions
(01923) 236906
www.becker.uk.com
Supply a range of sliding walls from concertina solutions to folding glazed doors.

Bisque
244 Belsize Road
London NW6 4BT
(020) 7328 2225
www.bisque.co.uk
Vertical radiators and wall-hung hoops.

BoConcept
158 Tottenham Court Road
London W1T 7NH
and branches
(020) 7388 2447
www.boconcept.co.uk
Stylish modular sofas, shelving and cabinets.

The Conran Shop
Michelin House
81 Fulham Road
London SW3 6RD
(020) 7589 7401
www.conranshop.co.uk
Good for modular furniture and storage.

Dorma
(01462) 477600
www.dorma-uk.co.uk
Frameless glass sliding, folding and revolving doors; also partitions and fixings.

DR Services (London)
(01279) 445277
www.drservices.co.uk
Sliding, stacking, and folding frameless glass doors and partitions. Can also supply fixings for wood and metal.

Habitat
(0870) 4115501 for branches
www.habitat.net
Broad range of compact and modular furniture.

Häfele
(01788) 542020
www.hafele.com
Architectural ironmongers who supply everything for sliding doors, as well as handles and fixings, foldaway beds and kitchen furniture.

Heal's
196 Tottenham Court Road
London W1T 7LQ
(020) 7636 1666
www.heals.co.uk
Stylish contemporary furniture and storage.

The Holding Company
241–245 Kings Road
London SW3 5EL
(020) 7352 1600
Call (020) 8445 2888
for mail order.
www.theholding company.co.uk
Furniture and accessories.

IKEA
(0845) 3551141 for branches.
www.ikea.com/gb
Good for compact furniture, kitchens and storage.

Inflate
1 Helmsley Place
London E8 3SB
(020) 7249 3034
www.inflate.co.uk
Makers of the ingenious Snoozy bed (see page 98).

The Institution of Structural Engineers
11 Upper Belgrave Street
London SW1X 8BH
(020) 7235 4535
www.istructe.org.uk
Give online referral for engineers in your area.

Ligne Roset
23–25 Mortimer Street
London W1T 3JE
(020) 7323 1248
www.ligne-roset-westend.co.uk
Good for sofabeds and dual-purpose furniture.

The London Wallbed Company
(020) 8896 3757
www.wallbed.co.uk
Huge range of wall beds. Also offer a design and installation service.

Nu-Heat
(0800) 7311976
www.nu-heat.co.uk
This company supplies underfloor heating and can recommend installers.

Pellfold Parthos Ltd
(01628) 773353
www.designs4space.com
Folding and sliding doors and partitions.

Purves & Purves
25–27 George Street
London W1U 3QA
(020) 7486 3200
Call (020) 8893 4000
for mail order.
www.purves.co.uk
Streamlined modern furniture and storage.

Real Flame
80 New Kings Road
London SW6 4LT
(020) 7731 2704
www.realflame.co.uk
Supply and install hole-in-the-wall fireplaces.

Royal Institute of British Architects Clients' Advisory Service
66 Portland Place
London W1B 1AD
(020) 7307 3700
www.architecture.com
Holds database of all RIBA-registered architects.

Selfridges
400 Oxford Street
London W1A 1AB
(0800) 123400
www.selfridges.com
Good for well-designed modular modern furniture.

SKK Lighting
34 Lexington Street
London W1F 0LH
(020) 7434 4095
www.skk.net
Supply fluorescent strip lights (to hide behind furniture etc.) in many different colours and lengths.

The Wallbed Workshop
(020) 7924 5300
Call (020) 7924 1323 for a brochure.
www.thewallbed workshop.co.uk
Supply and install large range of horizontal and vertical wall beds in different finishes.

Velux
(0870) 1667676
www.velux.co.uk
Supply list of skylight stockists.

stockists in the US

ABC Carpet & Home
881 & 888 Broadway
New York, NY 10003
212 473 3000
www.abchome.com
*Home furnishings,
fabrics, carpets, and
design accessories.*

American Society of Heating, Refrigeration, and Air Conditioning Engineers Inc.
17191 Tullie Circle NE
Atlanta, GA 30329
800 527 4723
www.ashrae.org

Anthropologie
375 West Broadway
New York, NY 10012
212 343 7070
Call 800 309 2500 for
your nearest store.
www.anthropologie.com
*Furniture and home
furnishings.*

California Closets
Call 800 274 6754 for
a store near you.
www.calclosets.com
*Custom-made clothes
storage to fit your space.*

Carlyle Custom Convertibles
1056 Third Avenue
New York, NY 10021
212 838 1525
www.carlylesofa.com
Convertible sofas.

Comfort Glow
800 446 1446
www.comfortglow.com
*Fire boxes, inset
fireplaces, radiant flame
heaters, and much more.*

The Conran Shop
407 East 59th Street
New York, NY 10022
866 755 9079
www.conranusa.com
*Cutting-edge design from
furniture to forks.*

Crate & Barrel
For a retailer near you,
call 800 967 6696.
www.crateandbarrel.com
*Good value furniture and
accessories with style.*

Create-A-Bed
4735 Poplar Level Road
Suite 3
Louisville, KT 40213
877 966 3852
www.wallbed.com
*Kit wall beds to put
together yourself.*

Get a Quote
www.get-a-quote.net
*Labor and material cost
estimates for residential
construction projects,
using the National
Construction Estimator.*

IKEA
For a store near you, call
800 434 4532.
www.ikea.com/us
*Home basics at great
prices, including
assembly-kit furniture.*

Imperial Cal Products
425 Apollo Street
Brea, CA 92821
800 851 4192
www.imperialhoods.com
*Under-hood lighting for
kitchen countertops.*

Kalwall
1111 Candia Road
P.O. Box 237
Manchester, NH 03105
800 258 9777
www.kalwall.com
*Wall systems, curtain
walls, windows, standard
and custom skylights,
sloped glazing systems.*

Kichler Lighting
866 558 5706
www.kichler.com
*Any type of lighting,
including under-counter
fluorescents.*

MOMA Design Store
44 West 53rd Street
New York, NY 10022
800 447 6662
www.momastore.org
*Furniture, lighting,
kitchen, and tabletop
accessories by modern
designers including
Starck, Wright, and Vasa.*

National Closet Group
866 624 5463
www.nationalclosetgroup.com
*A network of the best
independent storage
design companies.*

The National Terrazzo and Mosaic Association
800 323 9736
www.ntma.com
*Find a contractor who can
lay chips in resin flooring
(for a look similar to Guy
Hills's), or create specific
mosaic designs.*

Pier 1 Imports
71 Fifth Avenue
New York, NY 10003
212 206 1911
www.pier1.com
*Home accessories
and furniture.*

Pottery Barn
For a store near you, call
888 779 5176.
www.potterybarn.com
*Everything from furniture
to decoration details.*

Priva-lite
www.sggprivalite.com
*Electrically switchable
obscured glass (similar to
that shown on page 93).*

Restoration Hardware
935 Broadway
New York, NY 10010
212 260 9479
www.restoration
hardware.com
*Some of the funkiest
home furnishings,
lighting, and accessories
you'll find.*

Smith & Noble
800 248 8888
www.smithandnoble.com
*Vertical and horizontal
shades and blinds in all
materials, Roman shades,
cornice boxes.*

Velux America Inc.
800 88 VELUX
www.veluxusa.com
*Velux windows and
skylights.*

Waverly
800 440 0680
www.waverly.com
*Decorative accessories
including fabric,
wallpaper, furniture,
paint, window
treatments, and flooring.*

Your Complete Home
www.yourcompletehome.com
*Provides listings for
contractors in every state,
as well as helpful
information about
financing, hiring, and
do-it-yourself projects.*

architects & designers
whose work is featured in this book

**AB Construction
Contractor**
31 Aldbourne Road
London W12 0LW
+44 (0)20 8749 2044
Pages 96–97, 112 inset

**Bruce Bierman
Design, Inc.**
29 West 15 Street
New York, NY 10011
+1 212 243 1935
www.biermandesign.com
*Pages 81 l, 107, 113 l,
130–131 a, 130–131 b*

**Tito Canella
Canella & Achilli
Architects**
via Revere # 7/9
20123 Milano
Italy
+39 02 46 95 222
info@canella-achilli.com
www.canella-achilli.com
*Pages 1–2, 68, 69, 71 br,
75, 82, 98 a, 99, 113 l,
116, 128 c, 128 r, 129*

**Paul Collier
Architect**
209 rue St Maur
75010 Paris
France
+33 1 53 72 49 32
paul.collier@architecte.net
Pages 6, 74, 79 bl & r, 102

**Fabienne Couvert
Guillaume Terver
cxt sarl d'architecture**
12 rue Saint Fiacre
75002 Paris
France
+33 1 55 34 9850
www.couverterver-
architectes.com
Pages 4–5, 60–65

d-squared design
6b Blackbird Yard
Ravenscroft Street
London E2 7RP
+44 (0)20 7739 2632
dsquared@globalnet.co.uk
Pages 96–97, 112 inset

**Dune, Inc.
Furniture Fabrication**
88 Franklin Street
New York, NY 10013
+1 212 925 6171
Pages 24–31

**Helen Ellery
The Plot London
Interior Design**
77 Compton Street
London EC1V 0BN
+44 (0)20 7251 8116
helen@theplotlondon.com
www.theplotlondon.com
Pages 32–37, 73 r,

**Gavin Jackson
Architects**
50 Holland Park
London W11 3RS
+44 (0)20 7243 9000
www.gavinjackson
architects.com
*Pages 66–67, 70 b, 78, 79
al, 98 l*

**Guy Hills
Photographer**
+44 (0)7916 2610
+44 (0)7831 548068
guyhills@hotmail.com
www.guyhills.com
Pages 10–17

Interior Concepts
6 Warren Hall
Manor Road
Loughton
Essex IG10 4RP
+44 (0)20 8508 9952
+44 (0)7796 305133
jo_interiorconcepts
@hotmail.com
www.jointeriorconcepts.co.uk
*Pages 71 l, 72–73 l, 101 r,
108, 125 ar, 134–135*

**Jonathan Clark
Architects**
+44 (0)20 7286 5676
jonathan@jonathan
clarkarchitects.co.uk
www.jonathanclark
architects.co.uk
Pages 8–9, 38–45

**Clark Johnson
Lighting Consultant**
Johnson Schwinghammer
335 West 38th Street
New York, NY 10018
+1 212 643 1552
Pages 24–31

**Joseph Kerwin
Garden Consultant
La Buona Terra, Inc.**
261 West 22nd Street
New York, NY 10011
+1 212 229 2268
Pages 24–31

**David Khouri
Comma
Architecture, Interiors
& Furniture**
149 Wooster Street,
Suite 4NW
New York, NY 10012
+1 212 420 7866
info@comma-nyc.com
www.comma-nyc.com
Pages 24–31

**Mullman Seidman
Architects
Architecture & Interior
Design**
443 Greenwich Street,
2A
New York, NY 10013
+1 212 431 0770
wwww@mullmanseidman.com
*Pages 80 a , 81 r, 83,
86–87, 94*

François Muracciole Architect
54 rue de Montreuil
75011 Paris
France
+33 1 43 71 33 03
francois.muracciole
@libertysurf.fr
Page 128 l

Paul Daly Design Studio Ltd
11 Hoxton Square
London N1 6NU
+44 (0)20 7613 4855
studio@pauldaly.com
www.pauldaly.com
Pages 3, 52–59

Retrouvius Reclamation & Design
2A Ravensworth Road
Kensal Green
London NW10 5NR
+44 (0)20 8960 6060
www.retrouvius.com
Pages 10–17

Sage and Coombe Architects
(formerly Sage Wimer Coombe Architects)
12–15 Vestry Street,
5th Floor
New York, NY 10013
+1 212 226 9600
www.sageandcoombe.com
Page 88

Carla Saibene Womenswear collection, accessories and antiques Shop: Carla Saibene
via San Maurilio 20
Milano
Italy
+39 2 77 33 15 70
xaibsrl@yahoo.com
Pages 85, 100–101, 118–119, 126–127 a, 144

Seth Stein Architects
15 Grand Union Centre
West Row
Ladbroke Grove
London W10 5AS
+44 (0)20 8968 8581
admin@sethstein.com
www.sethstein.com
Page 93 al & ar

Shamir Shah
shahdesign@earthlink.net
Pages 46–51

Site Specific Ltd
305 Curtain House
134–146 Curtain Road
London EC2A 3AR
+44 (0)20 7689 3200
office@sitespecificltd.co.uk
www.sitespecificltd.co.uk
Pages 84, 90–91, 103, 125 b, 130 l

Nigel Smith
+44 (0)20 7278 8802
n-smith@dircon.co.uk
Page 93 b

Steven Learner Studio
307 Seventh Avenue
New York, NY 10001
+1 212 741 8583
+1 212 741 2180
www.stevenlearnerstudio.com
Page 125 al

Bruno Tanquerel Artist
2 Passage St Sébastien
75011 Paris
France
+33 1 43 57 03 93
Page 92

Todd Klein, Inc.
27 West 24th Street,
Suite 802
New York, NY 10010
+1 212 414 0001
todd@toddklein.com
www.toddklein.com
Pages 110–111, 112 main, 122–123, 127 b

3&Co
(formerly 27.12 Design Ltd)
333 Hudson Street
10th Floor
New York, NY 10014
+1 212 727 8169
www.threeandco.com
Pages 106, 120–121, 132

USE Architects
2nd Floor Temple Works
Brett Road
London E8 1JR
+44 (0)20 8986 8111
use.arch@virgin.net
www.usearchitects.com
Pages 89, 117, 124

Woodhams Landscape Ltd
378 Brixton Road
London SW9 7AW
+44 (0)20 7346 5656
stephen@woodhams.co.uk
www.woodhams.co.uk
&
Flowers
45 Elizabeth Street
Belgravia
London SW1W 9PP
+44 (0)20 7730 3353
Pages 70 a, 76–77, 80 b, 104–105, 109

With thanks to:
Hurford Salvi Carr
37–41 St John Street
London EC1M 4AN
+44 (0)20 7250 1012
sales@h-s-c.co.uk
www.hurford-salvi-carr.co.uk

picture credits

all photography by Chris Everard   **Key: a** = above,   **b** = below,   **r** = right,   **l** = left,   **c** = centre.

1–2 An apartment in Milan designed by Tito Canella of Canella & Achilli Architects; **3** Yuen-Wei Chew's apartment in London designed by Paul Daly Design Studio Ltd; **4–5** An apartment in Paris designed by architects Guillaume Terver and Fabienne Couvert of cxt sarl d'architecture; **6** An apartment in Paris designed by architect Paul Collier; **8–9** Architect Jonathan Clark's home in London; **10–17** Photographer Guy Hills's house in London designed by Joanna Rippon and Maria Speake of Retrouvius; **18–23** Ben Atfield's house in London; **24–31** Pemper and Rabiner home in New York, designed by David Khouri of Comma; **32–37** A house in London designed by Helen Ellery of The Plot London, paintings by Robert Clarke; **38–45** Architect Jonathan Clark's home in London; **46–51** A New York apartment designed by Shamir Shah. Paintings, Artist Malcolm Hill; **52–59** Yuen-Wei Chew's apartment in London designed by Paul Daly Design Studio Ltd. Paintings by Carol Robertson; **60–65** An apartment in Paris designed by architects Guillaume Terver and Fabienne Couvert of cxt sarl d'architecture; **66–67** A London apartment designed by architect Gavin Jackson; **68** An apartment in Milan designed by Tito Canella of Canella & Achilli Architects; **69** both Adèle Lakhdari's home in Milan; **70 a** Florist and landscape designer Stephen Woodhams's home in London, designed by architect Taylor Hammond; **70 b** A London apartment designed by architect Gavin Jackson; **71 br** An apartment in Milan designed by Tito Canella of Canella & Achilli Architects; **71 l** & **72–73 l** Jo Warman – Interior Concepts; **73 r** A house in London designed by Helen Ellery of The Plot London; **74** An apartment in Paris, designed by architect Paul Collier; **75** An apartment in Milan designed by Tito Canella of Canella & Achilli Architects; **76–77** Florist and landscape designer Stephen Woodhams's home in London, designed by architect Taylor Hammond. Kitchen by Camarque, dog sculpture by Justine Smith; **78** & **79 al** A London apartment designed by architect Gavin Jackson; **79 bl** & **r** An apartment in Paris designed by architect Paul Collier; **80** a John Kifner's apartment in New York, designed by Mullman Seidman Architects; **80 b** Florist and landscape designer Stephen Woodhams's home in London, designed by architect Taylor Hammond; **81 l** Central Park West Residence, New York City designed by Bruce Bierman Design, Inc.; **81 r** Peter and Nicole Dawes's apartment, designed by Mullman Seidman Architects; **82** An apartment in Milan designed by Tito Canella of Canella & Achilli Architects; **83** Peter and Nicole Dawes's apartment, designed by Mullman Seidman Architects; **84** An actor's London home designed by Site Specific; **85** Fashion designer Carla Saibene's home in Milan; **86–87** An apartment in New York, designed by Mullman Seidman Architects; **88** Bob & Maureen Macris' apartment on Fifth Avenue in New York designed by Sage Wimer Coombe Architects; **89** An apartment in London designed by Jo Hagan of Use Architects; **90–91** An actor's London home designed by Site Specific;**92** An apartment in Paris designed by Bruno Tanquerel; **93 al** & **ar** John Eldridge's loft apartment in London designed by Seth Stein; **93 b** Architect Nigel Smith's apartment in London; **94** Monique Witt and Steven Rosenblum's apartment in New York, designed by Mullman Seidman Architects; **95** One New Inn Square, a private dining room and home of chef David Vanderhook, all enquiries 020 7729 3645; **96–97** Programmable House in London, designed by d-squared; **98 b** A London apartment designed by architect Gavin Jackson; **98 a–99** An apartment in Milan designed by Tito Canella of Canella & Achilli Architects; **100–101** Fashion designer Carla Saibene's home in Milan; **101 r** Jo Warman – Interior Concepts; **102** An apartment in Paris, designed by architect Paul Collier; **103** An actor's London home designed by Site Specific; **104–105** Florist and landscape designer Stephen Woodhams's home in London, designed by architect Taylor Hammond; **106** Apartment of Amy Harte Hossfeld and Martin Hossfeld; **107** Central Park West Residence, New York City designed by Bruce Bierman Design, Inc.; **108** Jo Warman – Interior Concepts; **109** Florist and landscape designer Stephen Woodhams's home in London, designed by architect Taylor Hammond; **110–111, 112 main** Todd Klein's New York apartment designed by Todd Klein, Inc.; **112 inset** Programmable House in London, designed by d-squared; **113 l** An apartment in Milan designed by Tito Canella of Canella & Achilli Architects; **113 r** Central Park West Residence, New York City designed by Bruce Bierman Design, Inc.; **114–115** Mark Weinstein's apartment in New York designed by Lloyd Schwan; **116** Adèle Lakhdari's home in Milan; **117** An apartment in London designed by Jo Hagan of Use Architects; **118–119** Fashion designer Carla Saibene's home in Milan; **120–121** Apartment of Amy Harte Hossfeld and Martin Hossfeld; **122–123** Todd Klein's New York apartment designed by Todd Klein, Inc.; **124** An apartment in London designed by Jo Hagan of Use Architects; **125 al** An apartment in New York designed by Steven Learner; **125 ar** Jo Warman – Interior Concepts; **125 b** An actor's London home designed by Site Specific; **126–127 a** Fashion designer Carla Saibene's home in Milan; **127 b** Todd Klein's New York apartment designed by Todd Klein, Inc.; **128 l** François Muracciole's apartment in Paris; **128 c, 128 r** & **129** An apartment in Milan designed by Tito Canella of Canella & Achilli Architects; **130 l** An actor's London home designed by Site Specific; **130–131 a** & **b** Central Park West Residence, New York City designed by Bruce Bierman Design, Inc.; **132** Apartment of Amy Harte Hossfeld and Martin Hossfeld; **133** Mark Weinstein's apartment in New York designed by Lloyd Schwan; **134–135** Jo Warman – Interior Concepts; **144** Fashion designer Carla Saibene's home in Milan.

The author would like to thank Azby Brown for information about Japanese design.

index

page numbers in *italic* refer to captions and illustrations